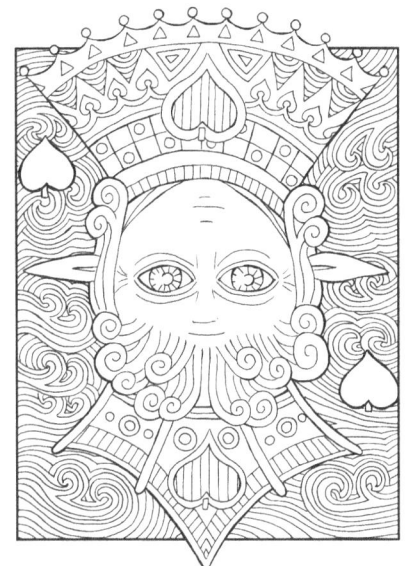
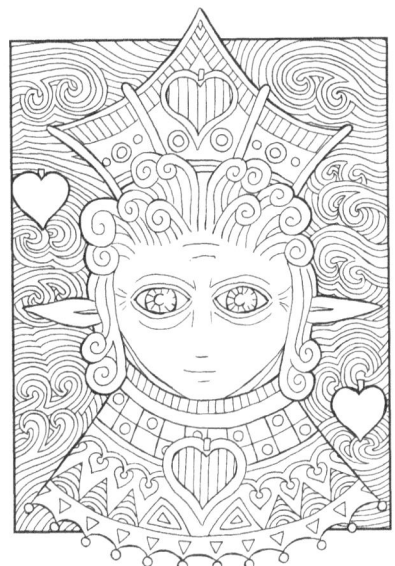

Multiview
ILLUSIONS COLORING BOOK

'TRICK SLATTERY

COLOR ARTIST:

_____

Multiview Illusions Coloring Book

Published in 2016 by
Tricksplace

ISBN: 978-0-9938669-1-3

Created by 'Trick Slattery
www.TricksPlace.com

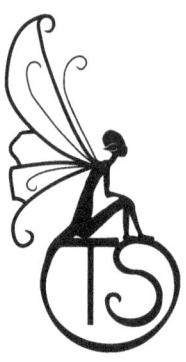

Thank You!

Thank you for your interest in coloring in the "multiview" illustrations that I've created for your enjoyment and relaxation. I started this book when I noticed that there weren't any other "multiview illusions" coloring books out there, and I thought that this could bring a whole new dimension to coloring - a first of its kind in the coloring book world.

This multiview illusions coloring book has 25 illustrations all hand-drawn and digitally edited by me ('Trick). Most are completely original ambiguous optical illusions, and others are inspired by classical illusions. I thought it would be best to have a good mix.

All illustrations can be seen in more than one way. I've created them with varying complexities, so if you are looking for a challenge you can choose a more intricate drawing with lots of nooks to color, or if you are looking for something quick or easy, a more simplistic page would be the way to go.

Each illustration has been duplicated for a total of 50 coloring pages (the duplicates are in the back half of the book), giving you a chance to color a different "view" of the same artwork or for a do-over.

There are different ways to go about coloring a multiview illusion page. Here are suggestions from the most relaxing to the most challenging:

- Don't think about the different views at all. Just pick up the pencils or other media and let your subconscious do most of the work. In the end, see if your mind went naturally to one view over another, or if there was more of a balanced view.

- Find the view that your mind naturally goes to and color that view in a way that stands out over the other.

- Look for the view your mind has a harder time recognizing (if there is one), and color that view in a way that makes it stand out over the easier view.

- Try to color the page in a way that both views work equally with the colors. This is a little more challenging as you need to keep both views in mind while coloring.

After you have completed coloring a page using one technique, you might want to use the duplicate page to color a different view. This can lead to some very interesting comparisons in which the same page looks completely different.

 SHARE YOUR COLORED WORK! After you have colored in a page, if you want to - scan it in and share it on social media with the hashtag of #tricksplace and #multiviewcoloring. This will make it easy for me and others to find. Please do not post or share uncolored pages. Also, join this dedicated facebook group and share there: facebook.com/groups/TricksPlaceColoring/

25 Illusions to color

17 entirely original illusions and 8 with ideas *inspired by classic illusions - all drawn in my unique quirky, strange, and whimsical style.

01 - Seahorse or chameleon?
02 - Queen of hearts or king of spades (elves)?
03 - Elephant or swan? *
04 - Donkey or seal? *
05 - Orangutan or monkey?
06 - Owl or parrots front the moon (or with large backs)?
07 - Turn that frown upside down - baby!
08 - Two bears holding hands or one big bear?
09 - Bird eating mouse or mouse in a canoe near a fish? *
10 - Jester cat or king fish?
11 - Egyptian bird or rhino?
12 - Moth on a tree, happy tree creature, or disgruntled tree creature?
13 - Mountain landscape or lion?
14 - Elf or troll chief?
15 - Two people facing each other, or one front view face behind a vase, or vase face? *
16 - Fish or lagoon creature?
17 - One big cat or two cats head to head?
18 - Dragon or frog? *
19 - Turn that clown, upside down.
20 - Strange bird or rabbit? *
21 - Penguin or caribou? *
22 - Young woman or old lady looking through a window? *
23 - Hairy caveman or tiny-head man with big hair?
24 - Mouse in fruit basket or pig creature with tongue out?
25 - Big-eared alien with a small robot or long eyed alien with a UFO?

* Inspiration

Ambiguous optical illusions can be found very early on in history. These works of art or concepts have paved the way in promoting new ways to see things. Some of the first flip optical illusions were created by Giuseppe Arcimboldo in the 16th century using fruit. Here are some inspirations for a few of my renditions: (03) loosely inspired by Salvador Dalí, (04) inspired by anonymous sketches, (09) closer to hand-drawn reproduction by Gustave Verbeek 1904, (15) inspired by Edgar Rubin 1915, (18) inspired by horse/frog anonymous sketch - 19th century, (20) inspired by Joseph Jastrow 1899, (22) closer to a hand drawn reproduction of anonymous 1888 German postcard.

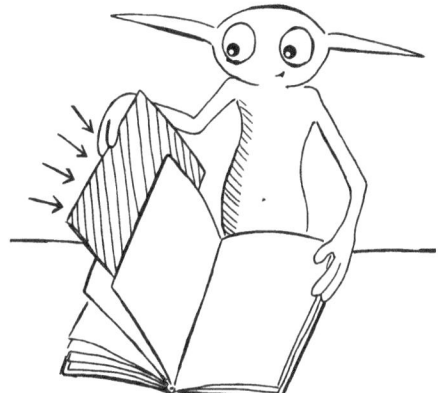

Though the illustrations are single-sided, you will still want to protect the pages under the one you are working with. Slide a blank sheet of paper between the page you are coloring and the next image underneath it. This will help protect the other pages from hard colored pencil indents, etc. If you use markers or gel pens you may want to use more than one page, or cardstock, as wet media may seep through to the next page.

I've left a large margin to make it easy to color the full image near the spine of the book. This also gives you room to cut out the page and frame it! If you are using an X-Acto knife to cut out a page, make sure to protect the pages underneath with cardboard or cardstock that you will not cut through.

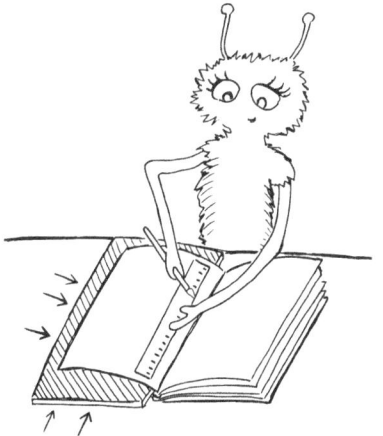

Test out how your media will appear on the paper used for this coloring book on the last "color test" page of the book. Not all coloring paper behaves the same, so testing first can help prevent unwanted results. That being said, don't worry too much, as I've provided duplicates of every coloring page, so if things don't go as planned you can always start again.

Most of all, have fun. There is no wrong answer! Coloring can have many relaxation and stress reduction benefits, so relax and just let your creativity flow. Keep in mind that a coloring book allows you to experiment and express yourself with color without the need to create the structure of the artwork. This allows a natural creative process, and after you have colored your first page you are now a "color artist". And like all artists you will see changes to the way you color as your style evolves.

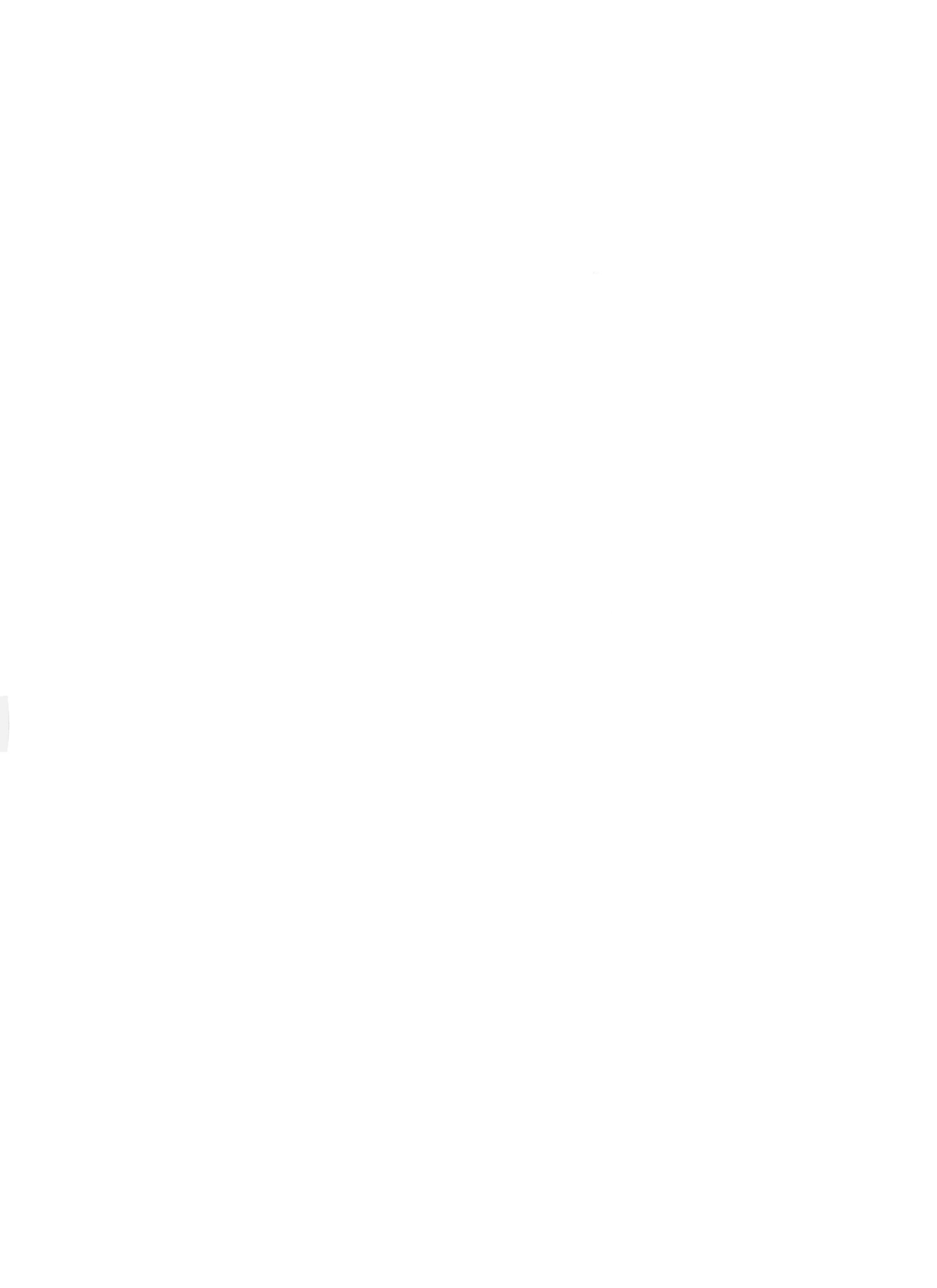

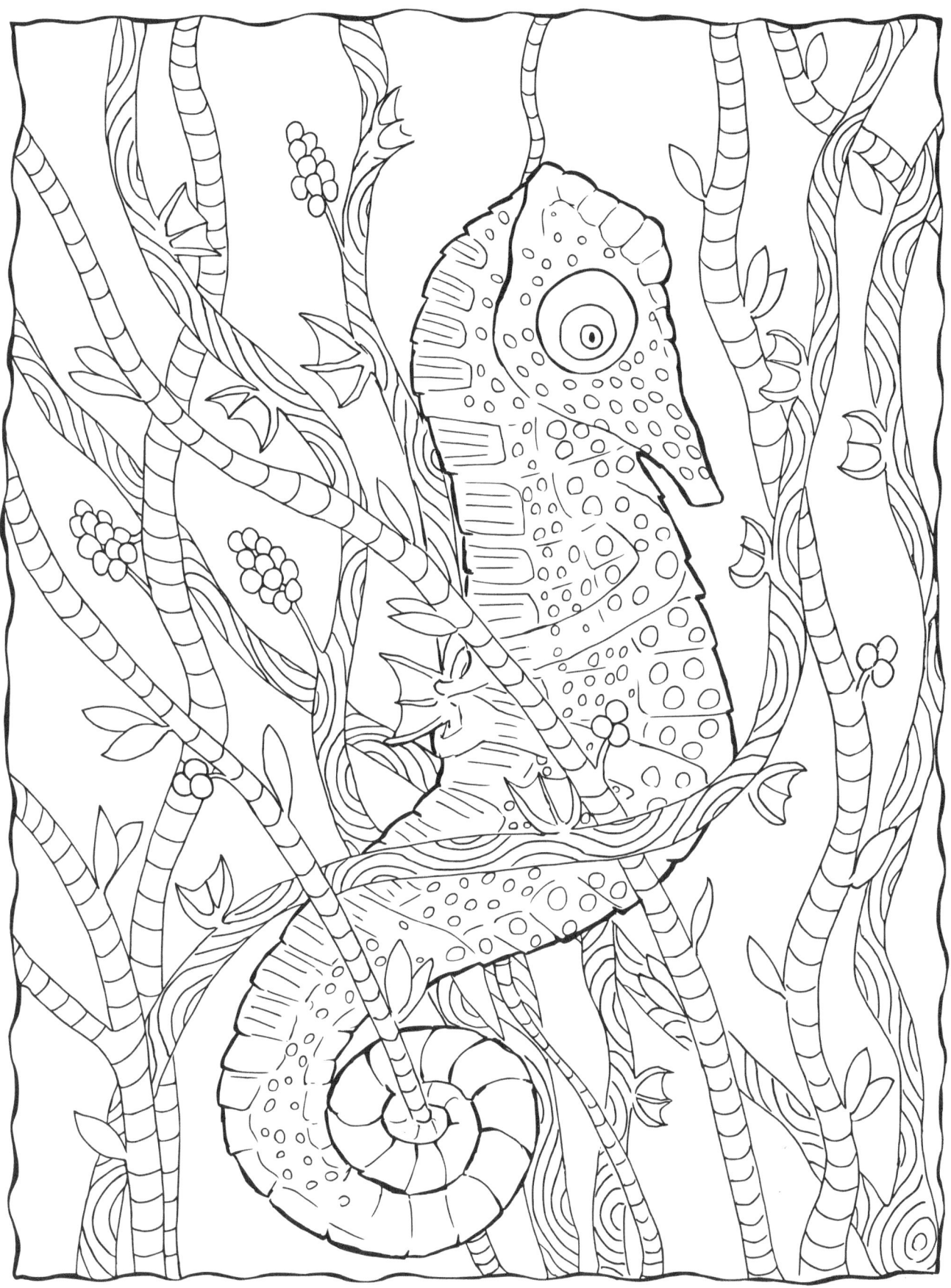

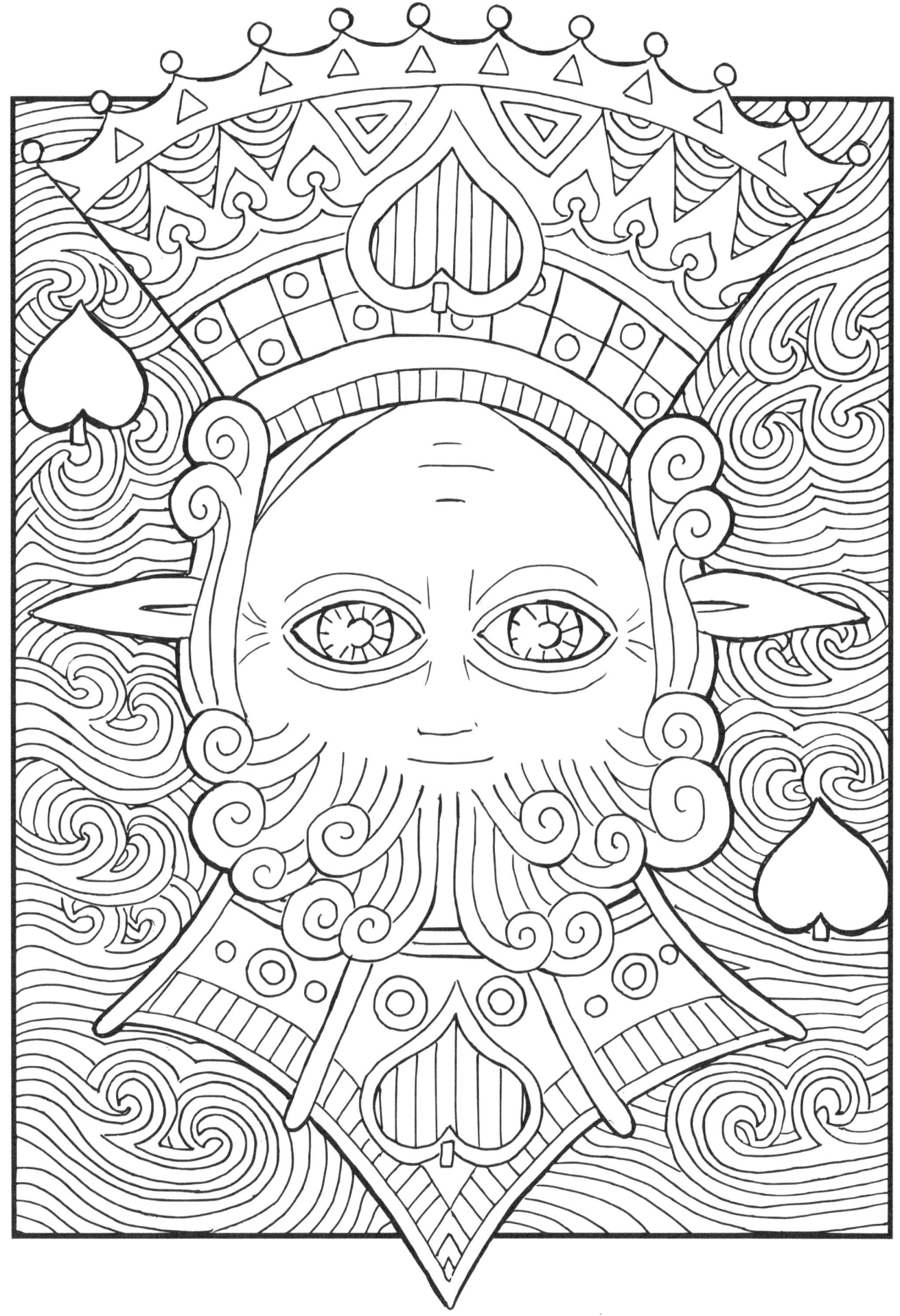

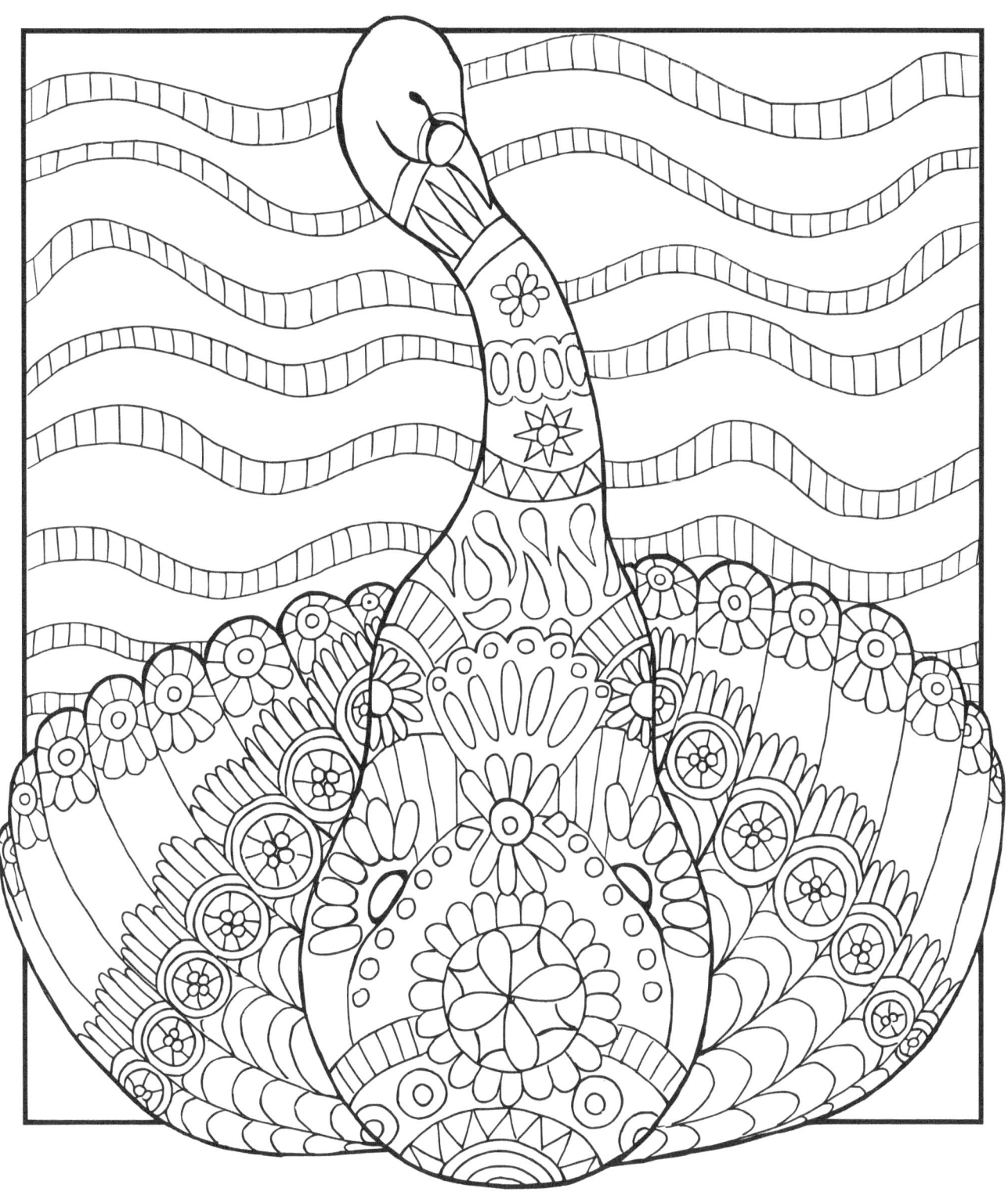

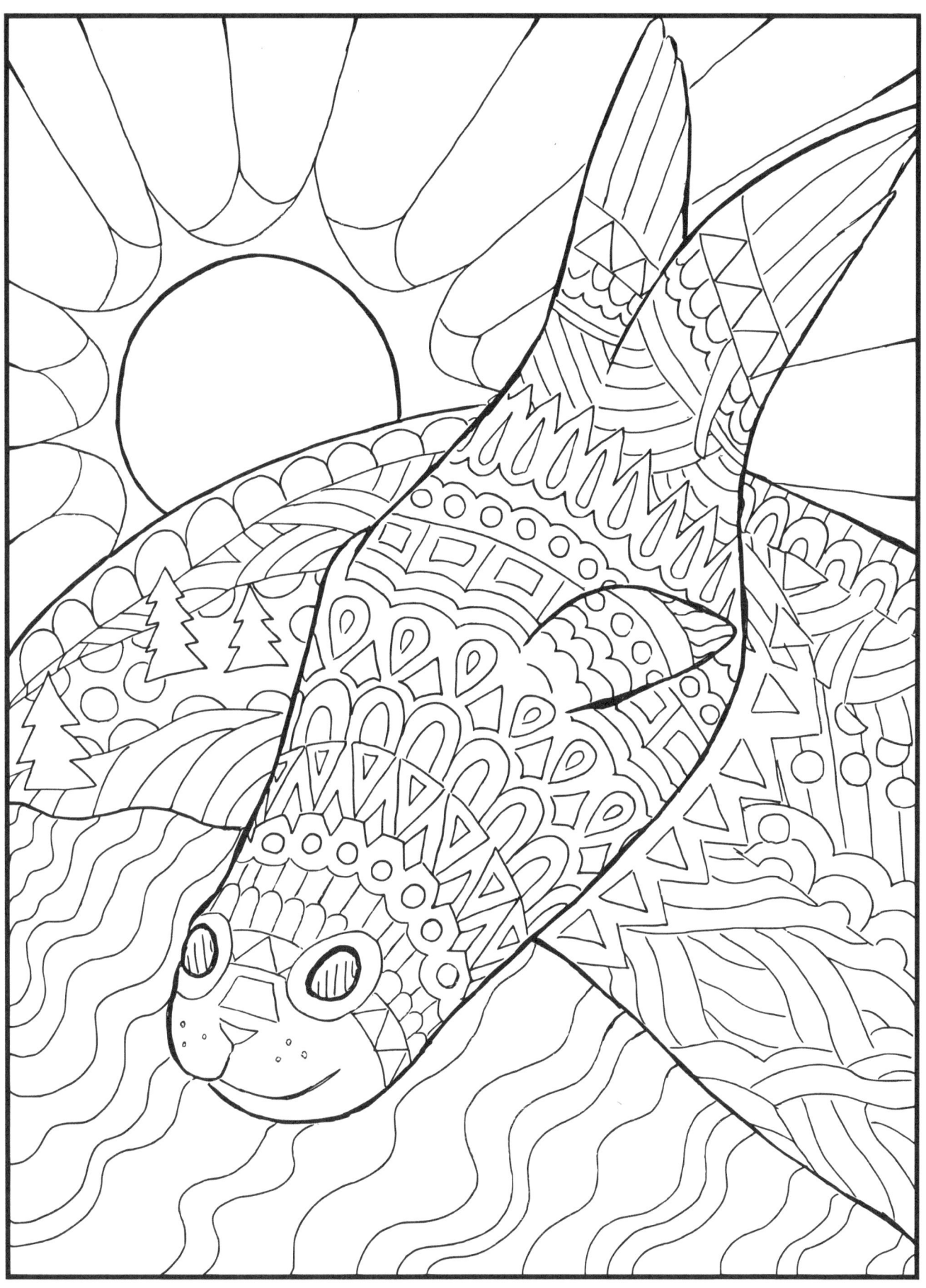

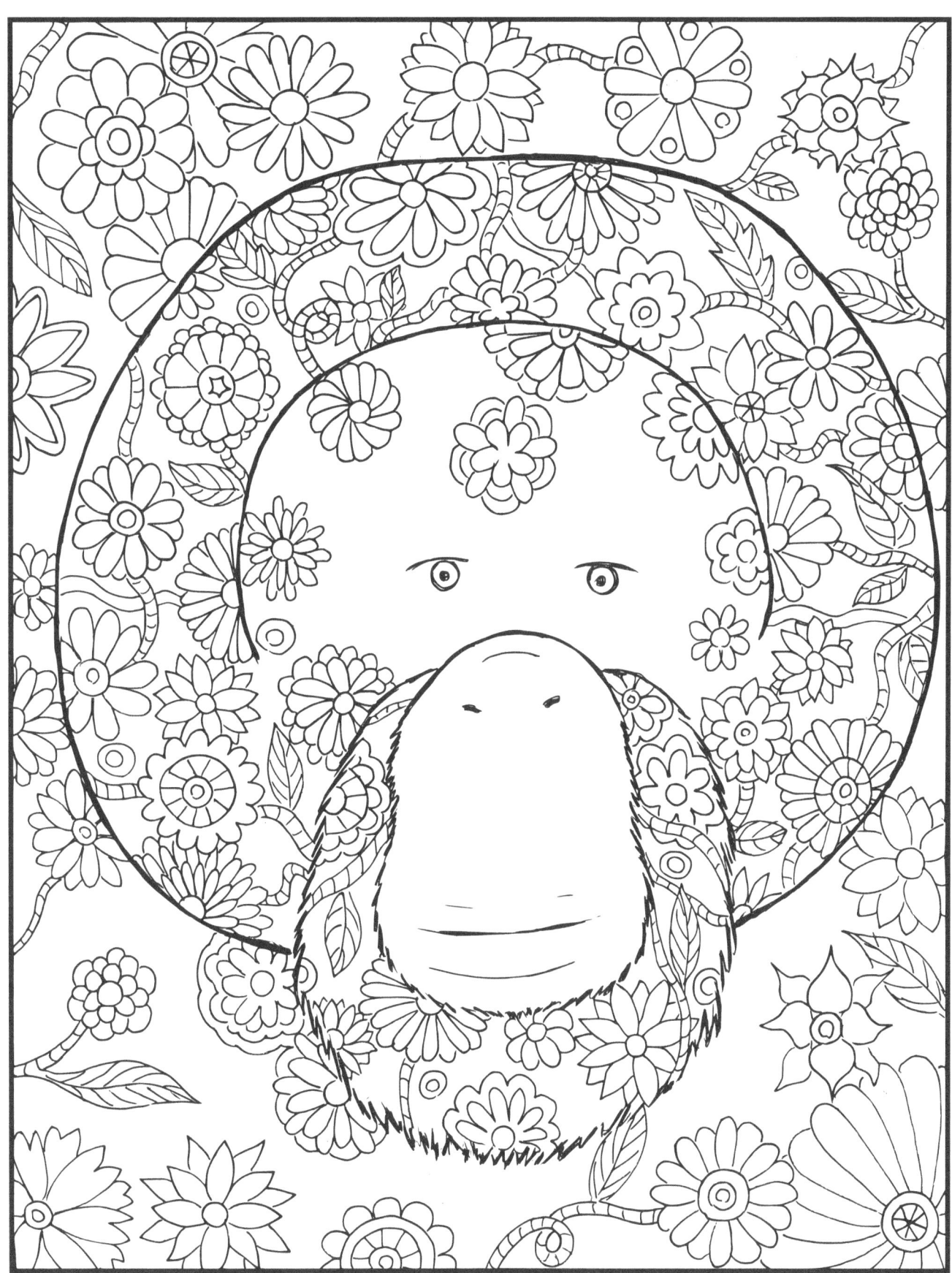

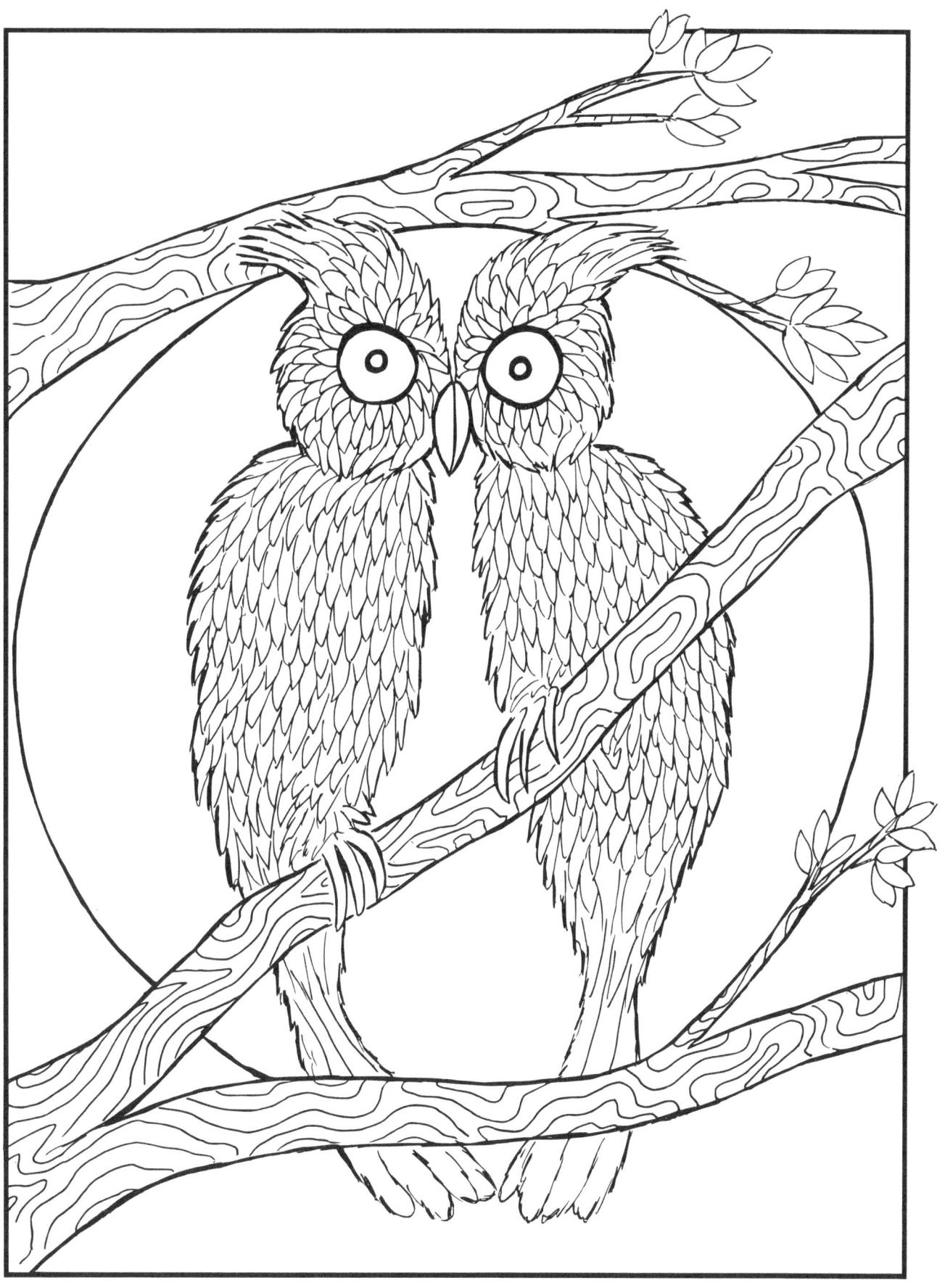

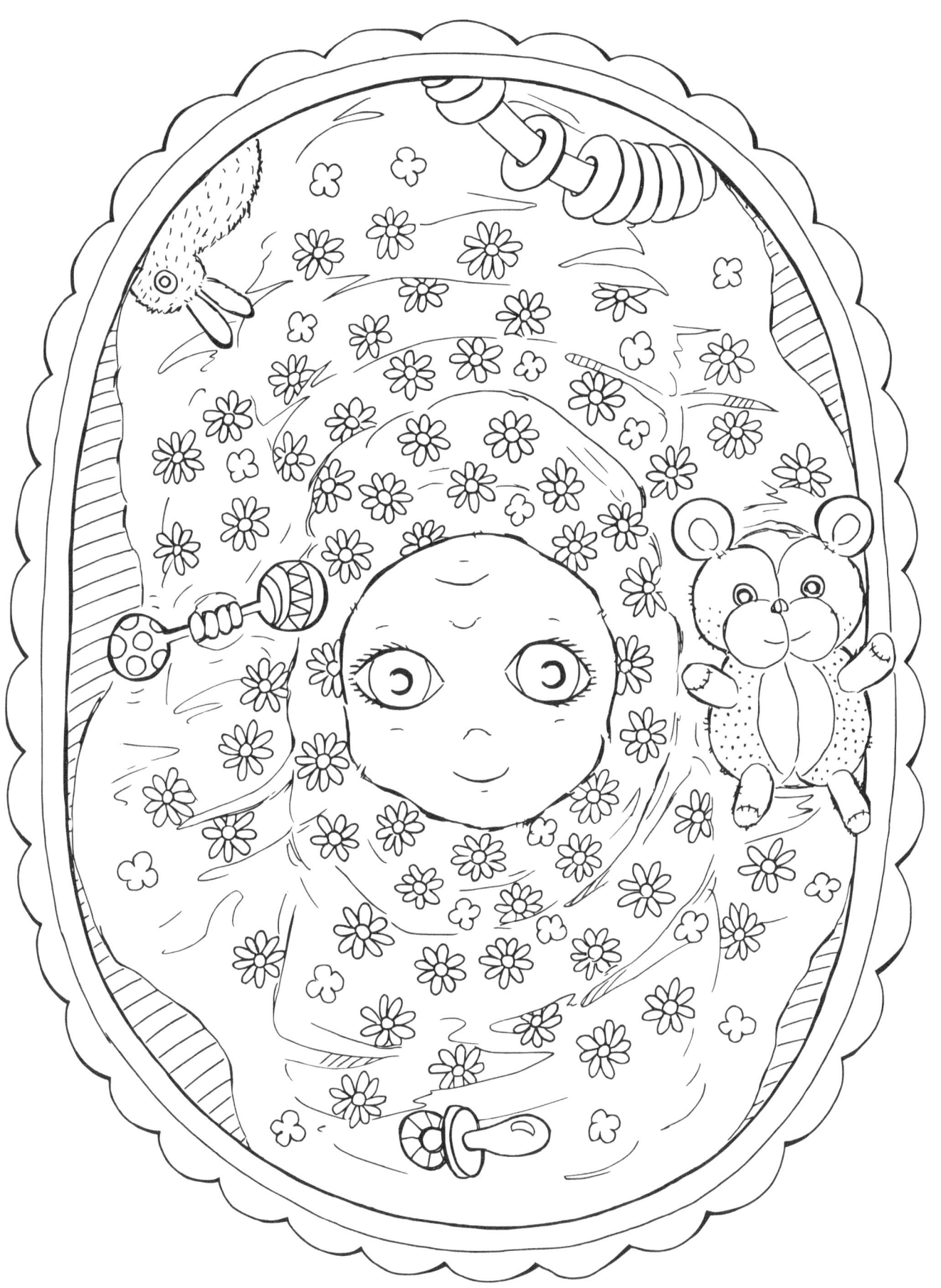

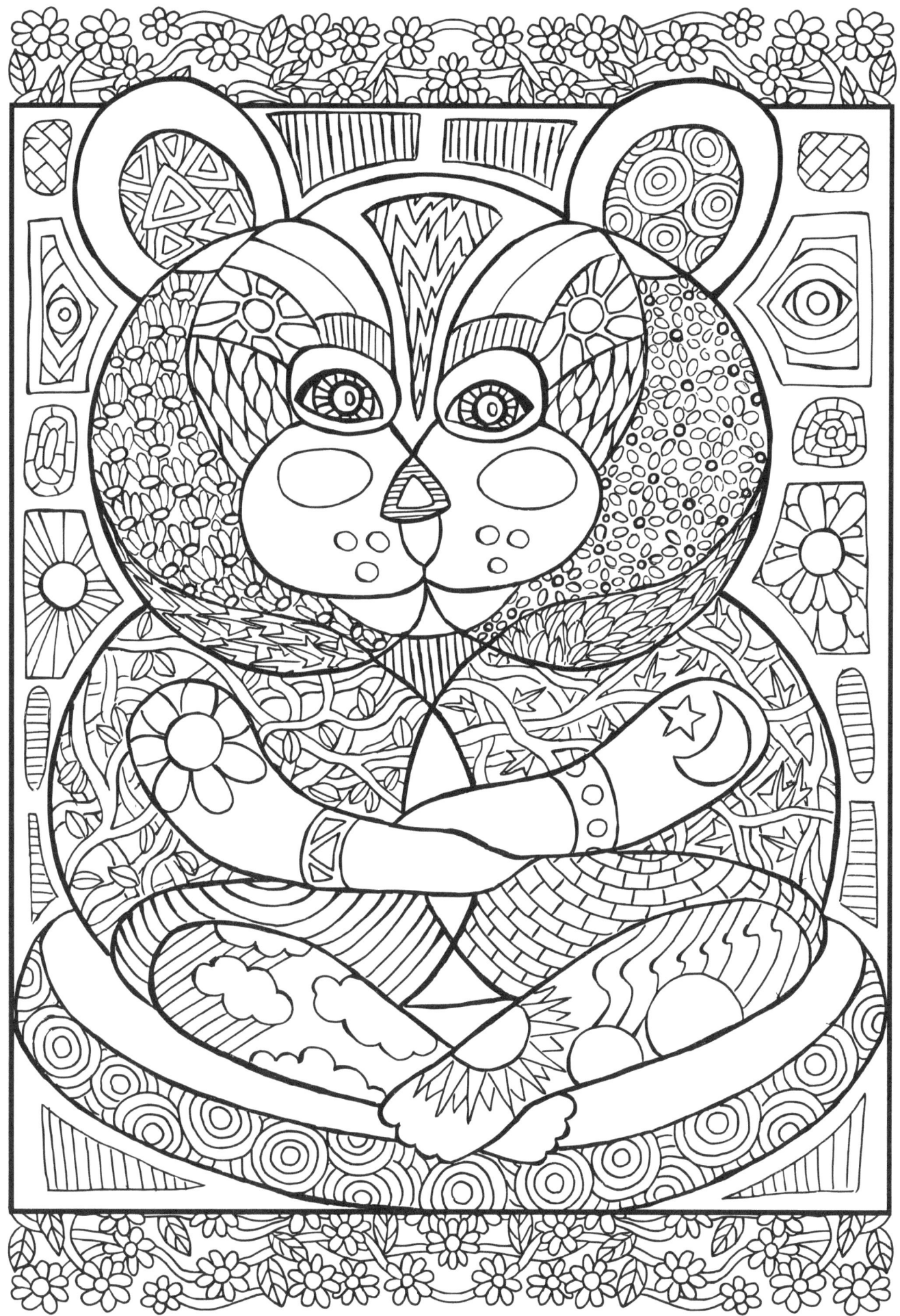

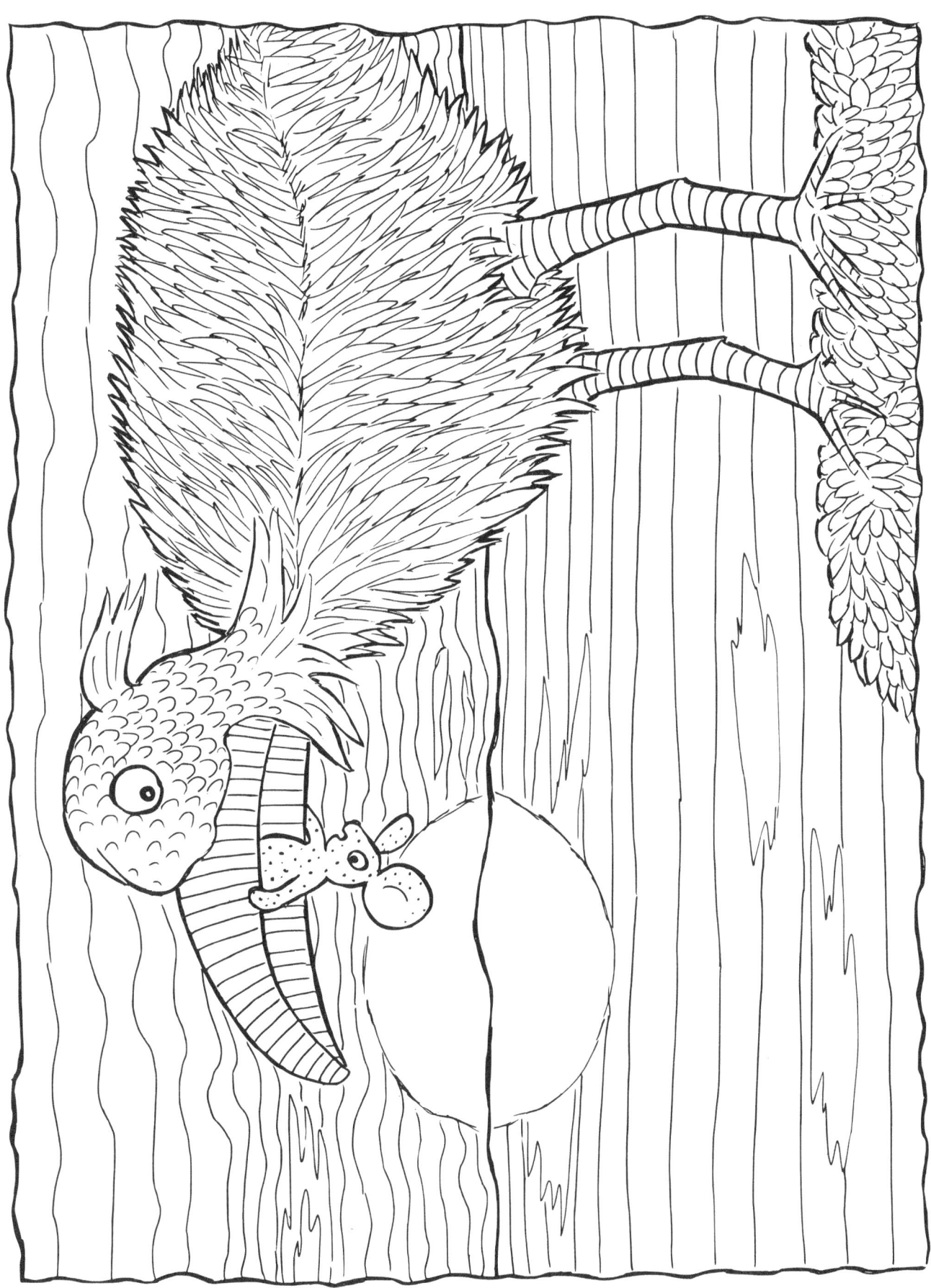

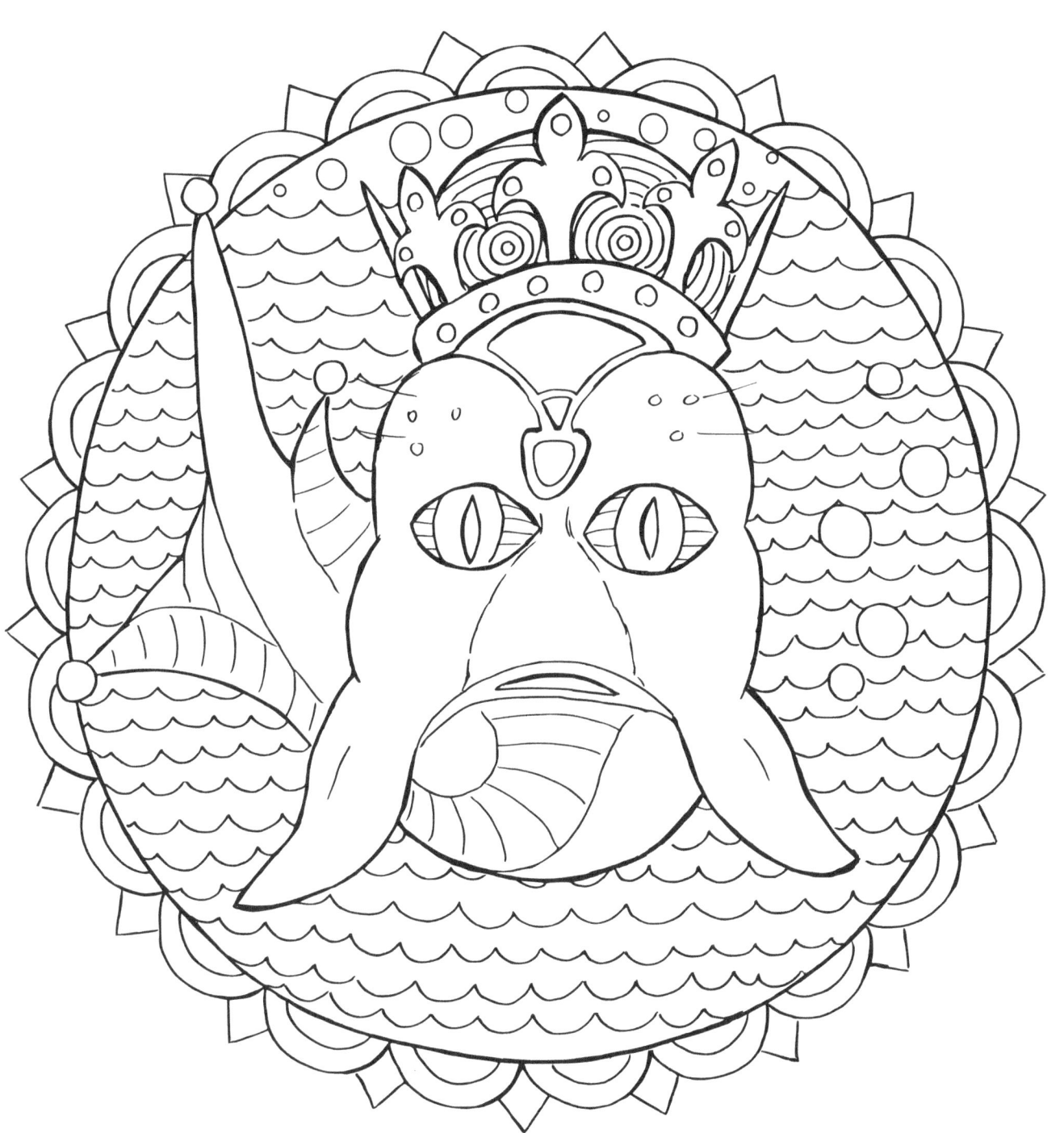

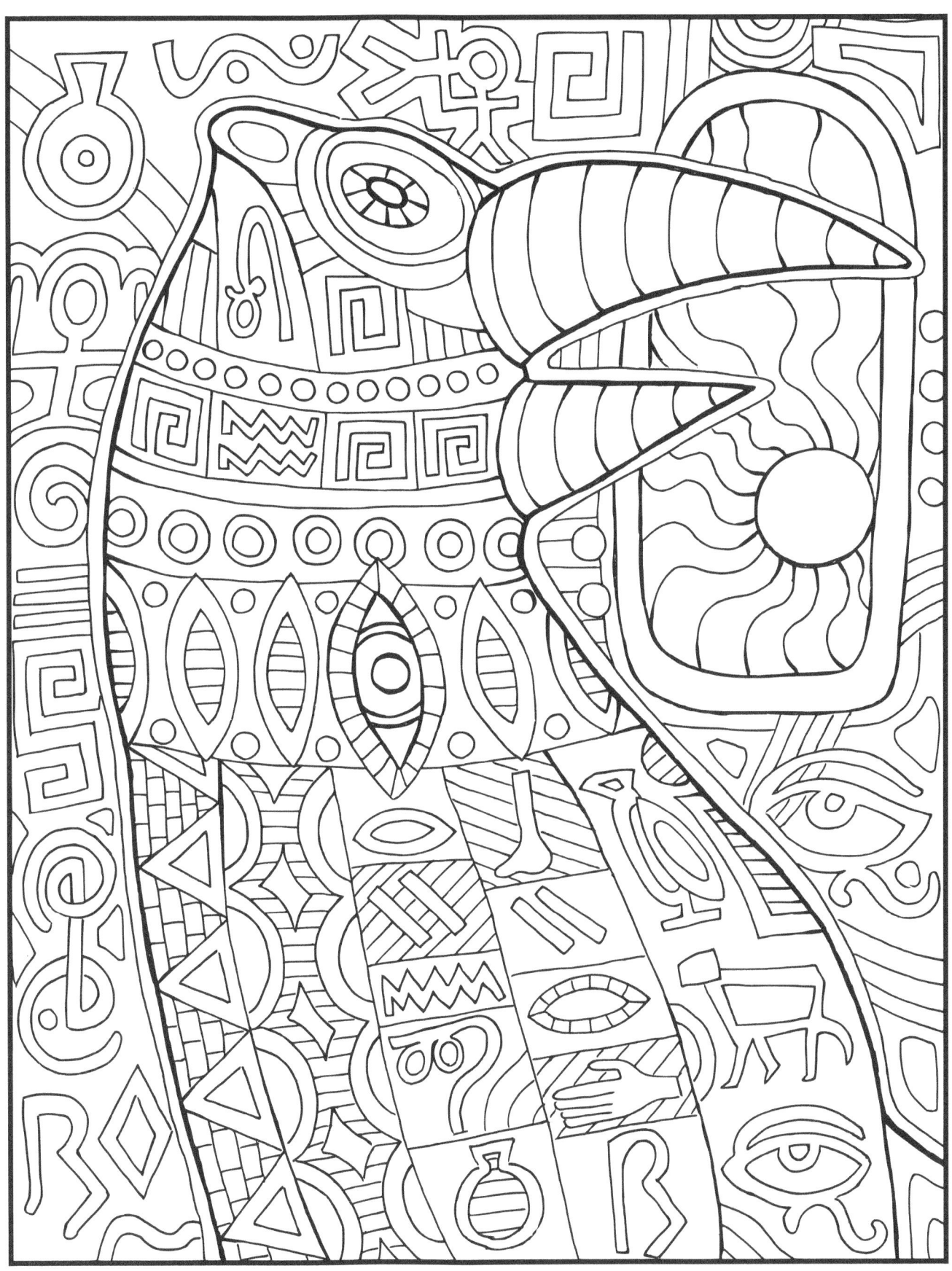

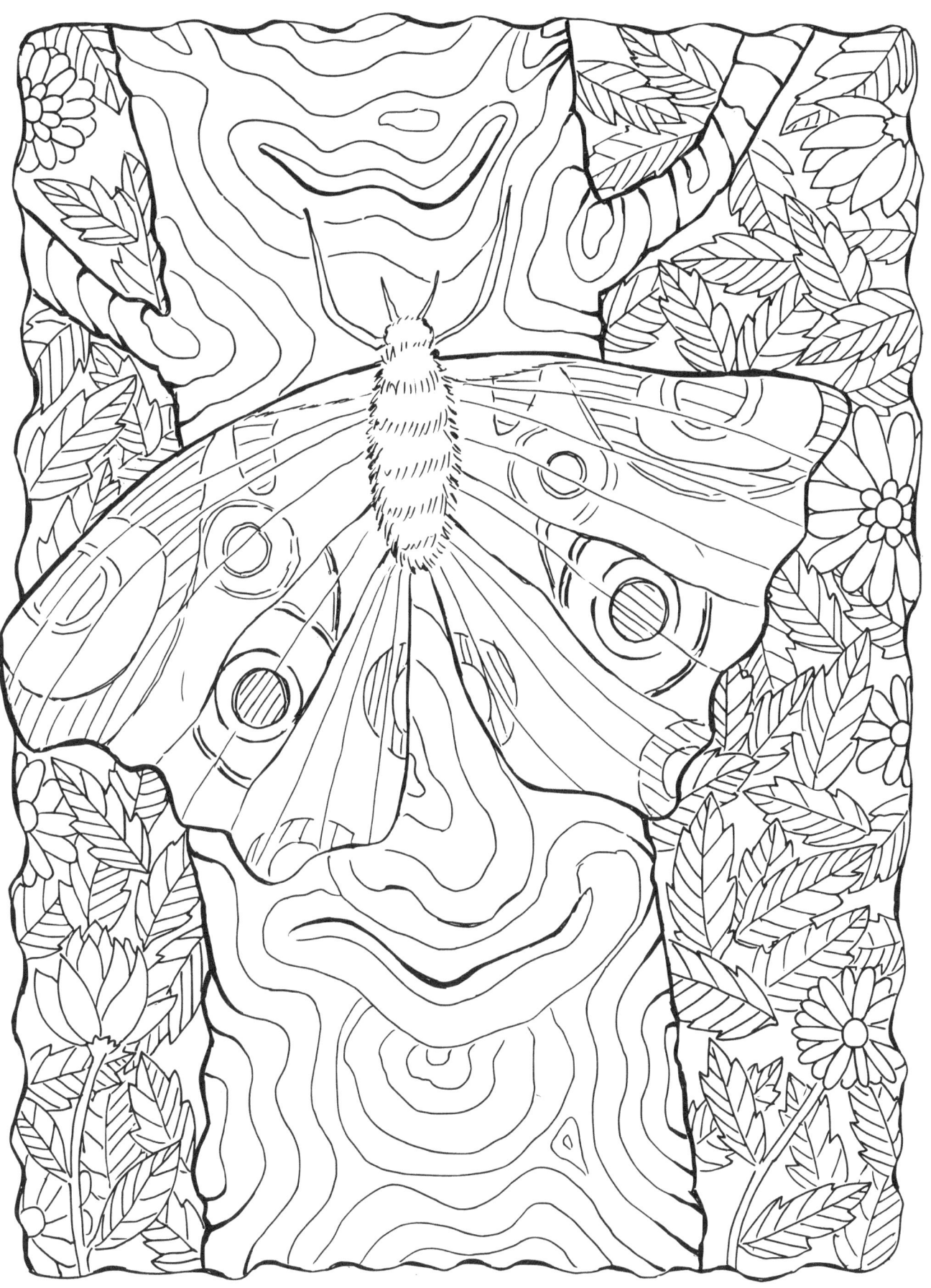

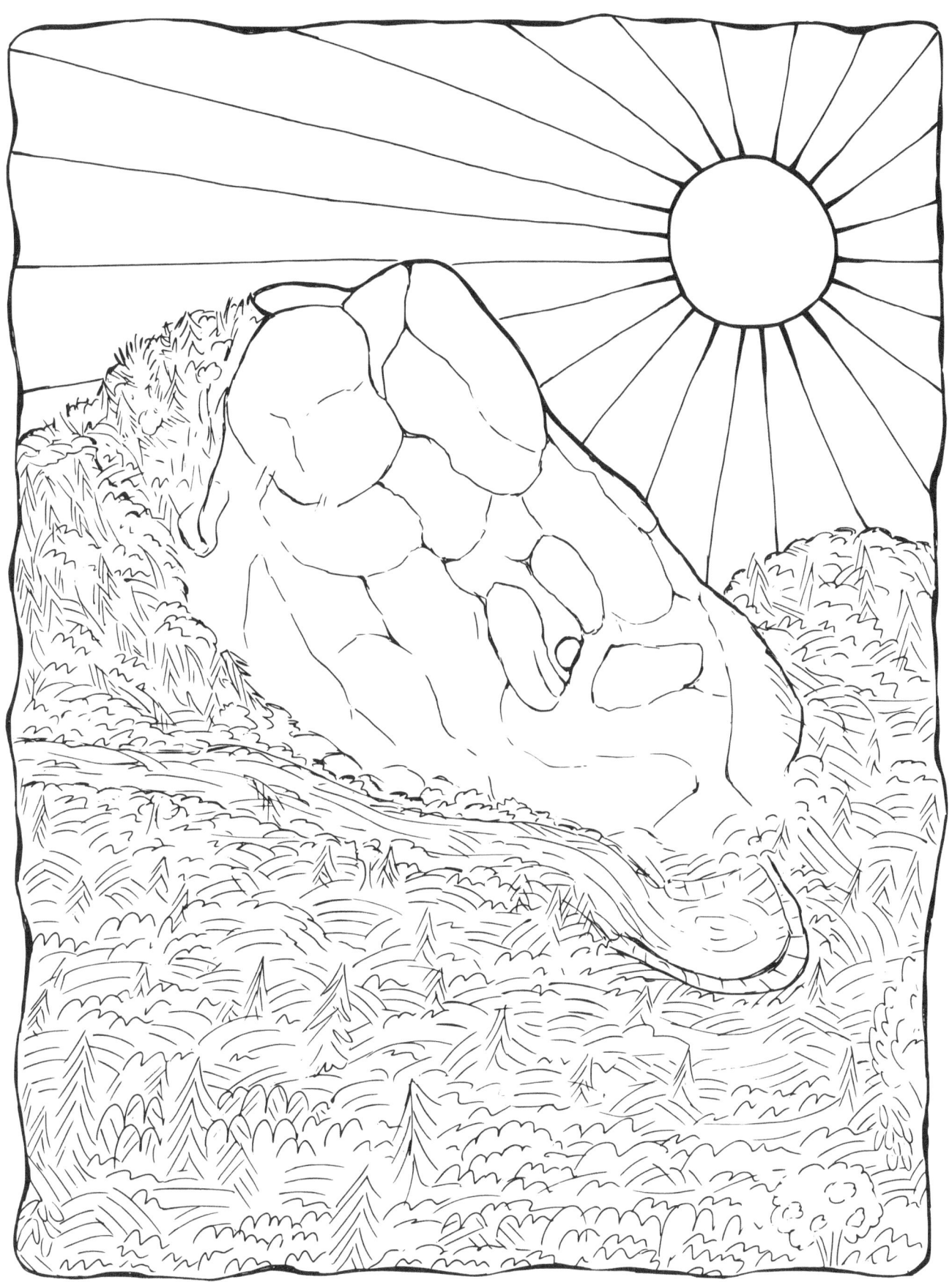

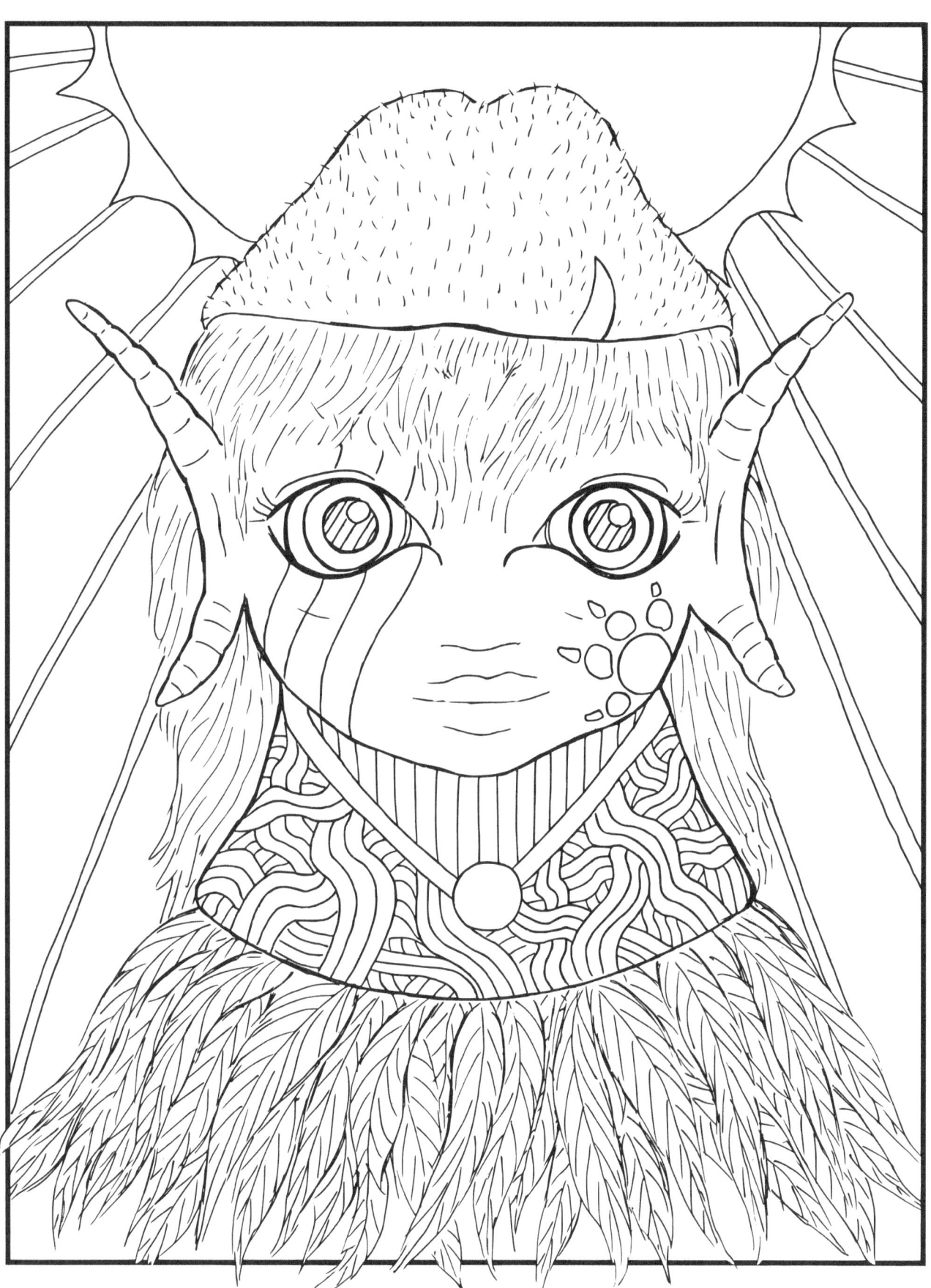

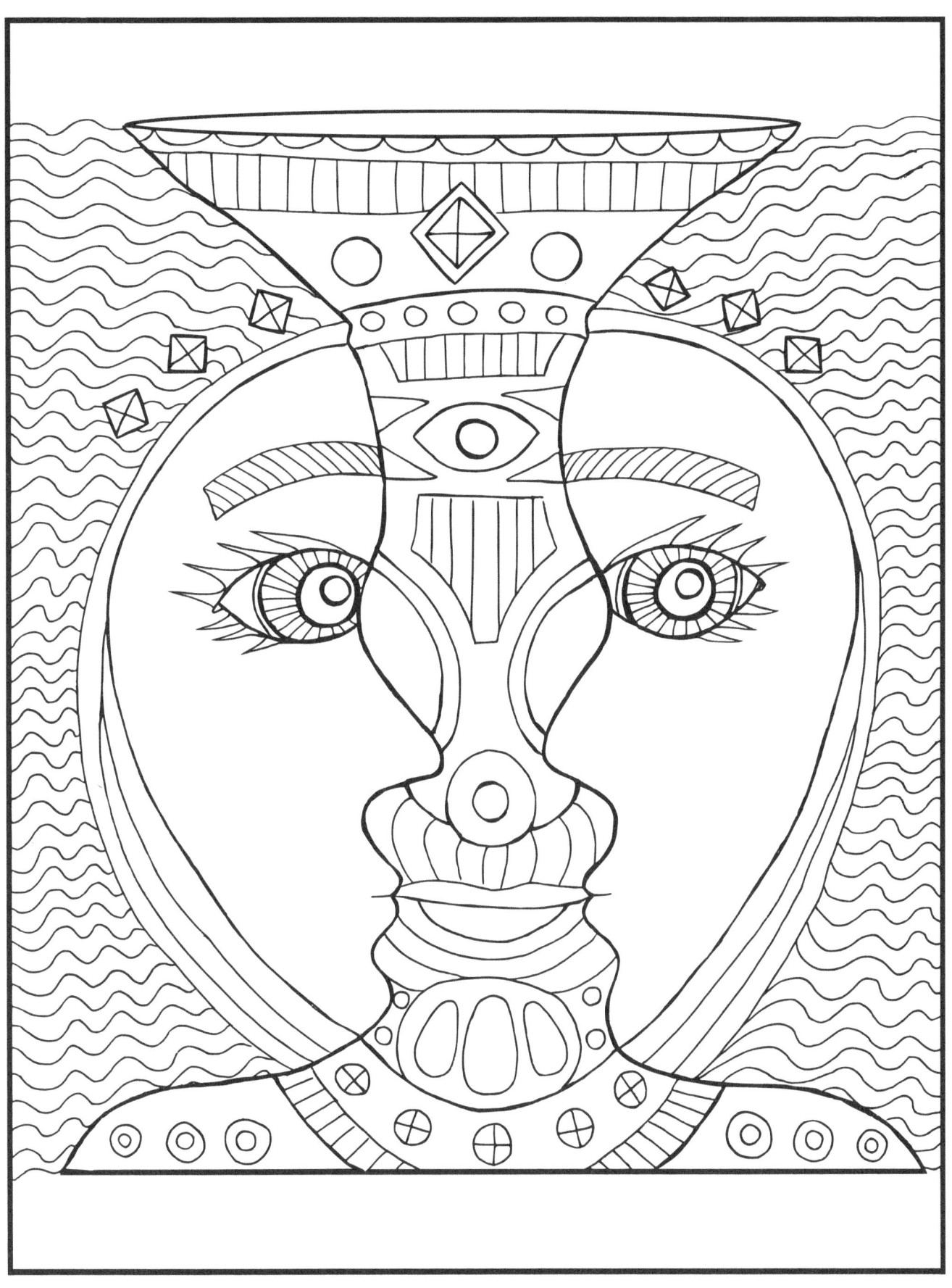

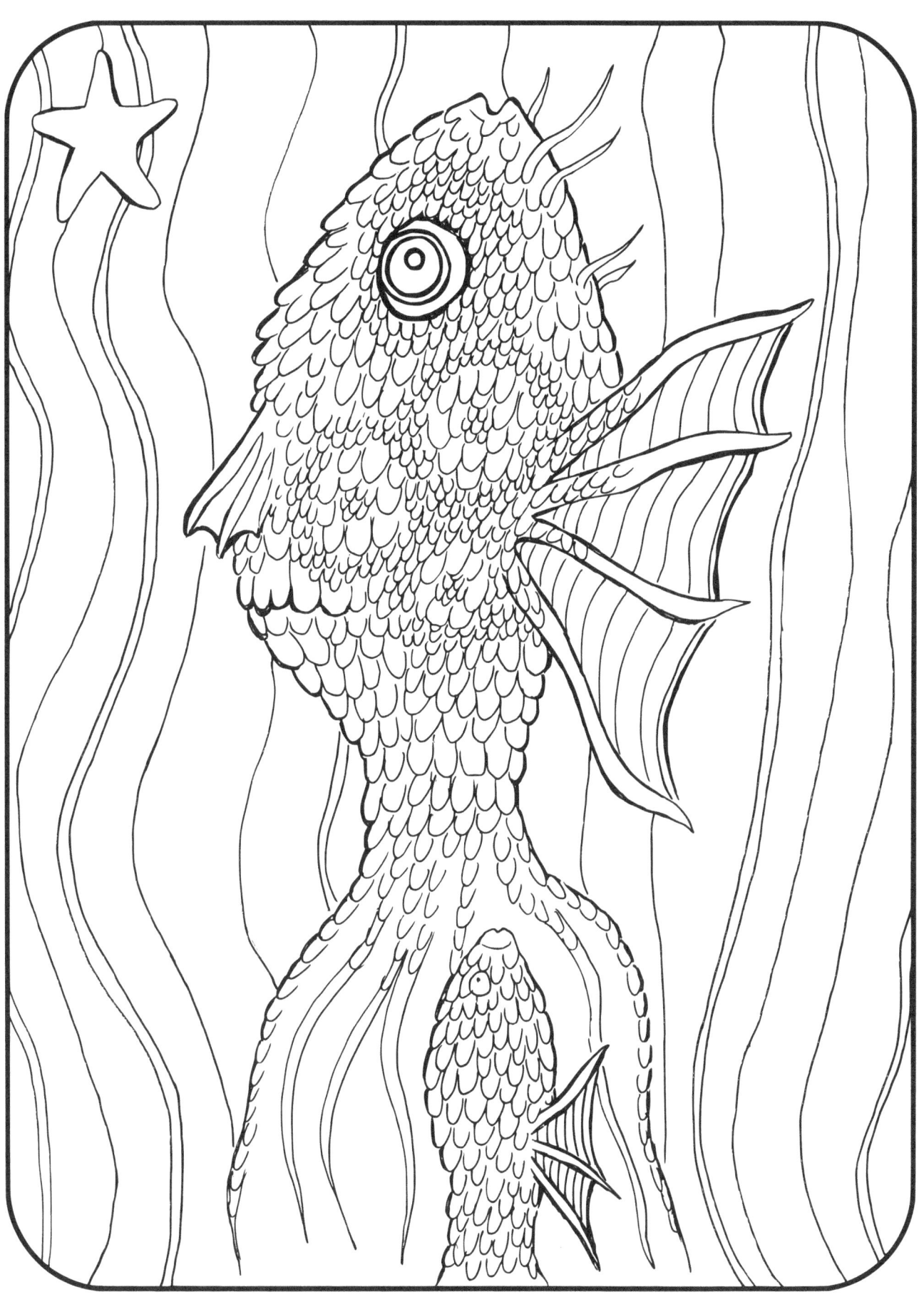

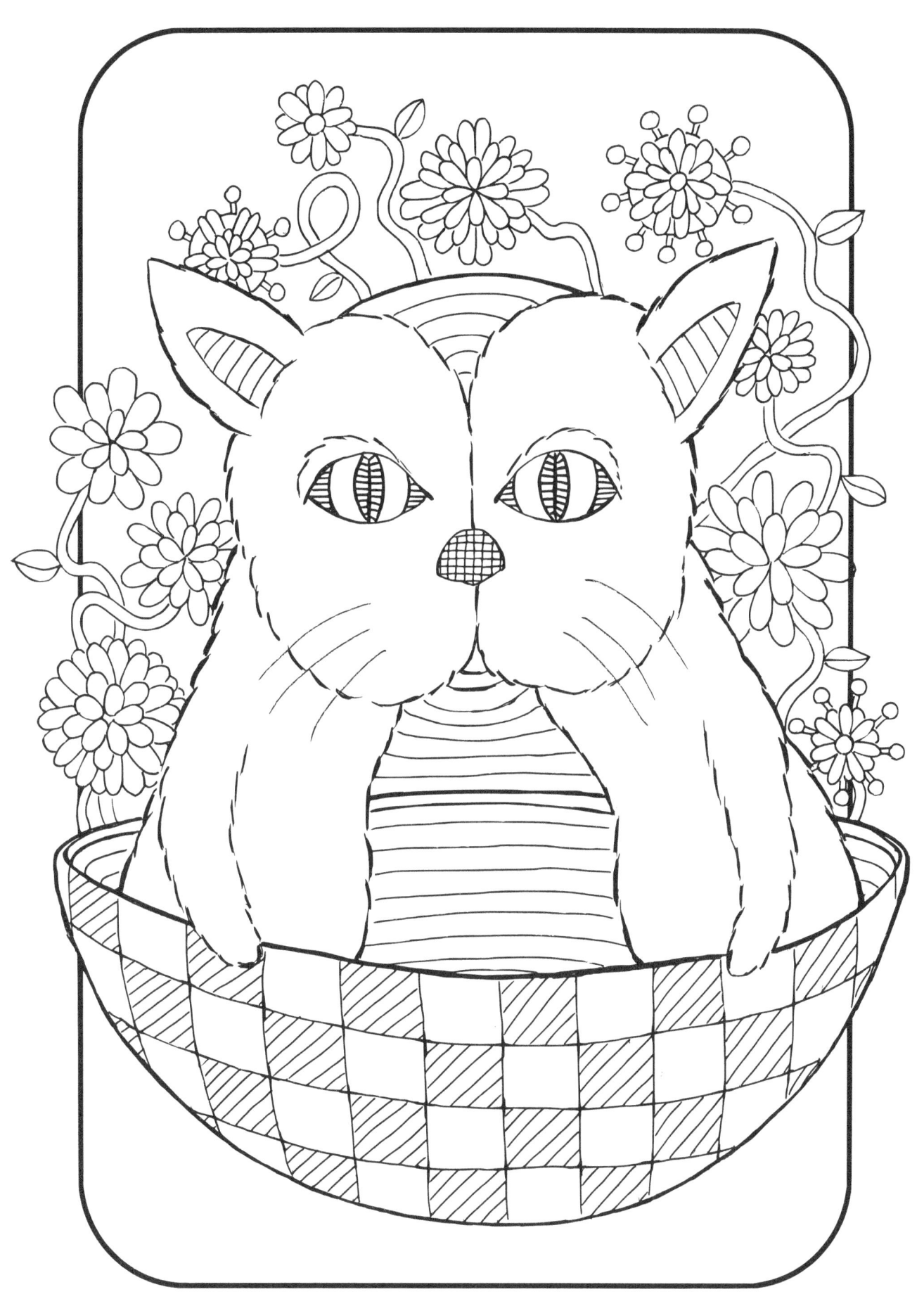

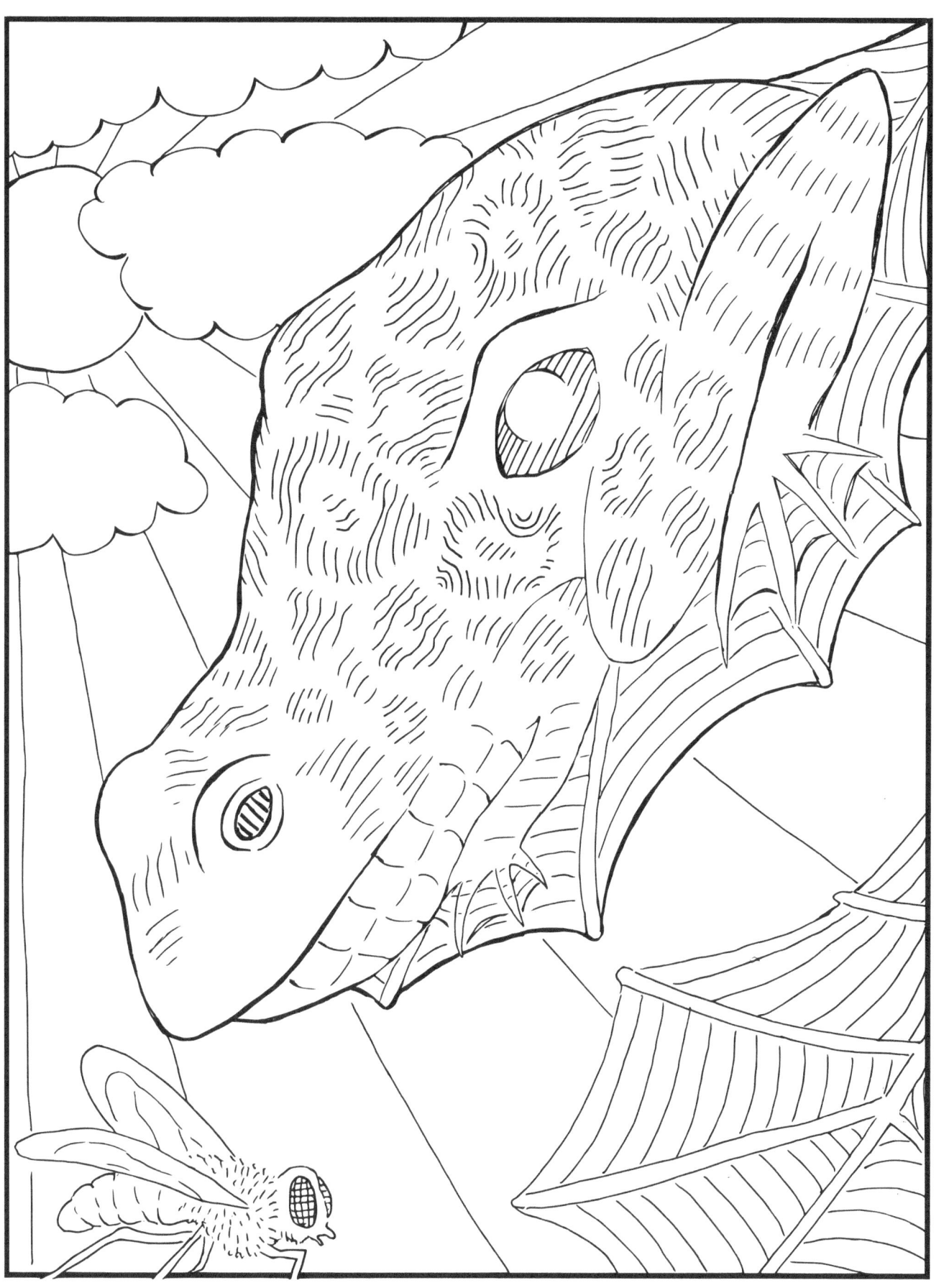

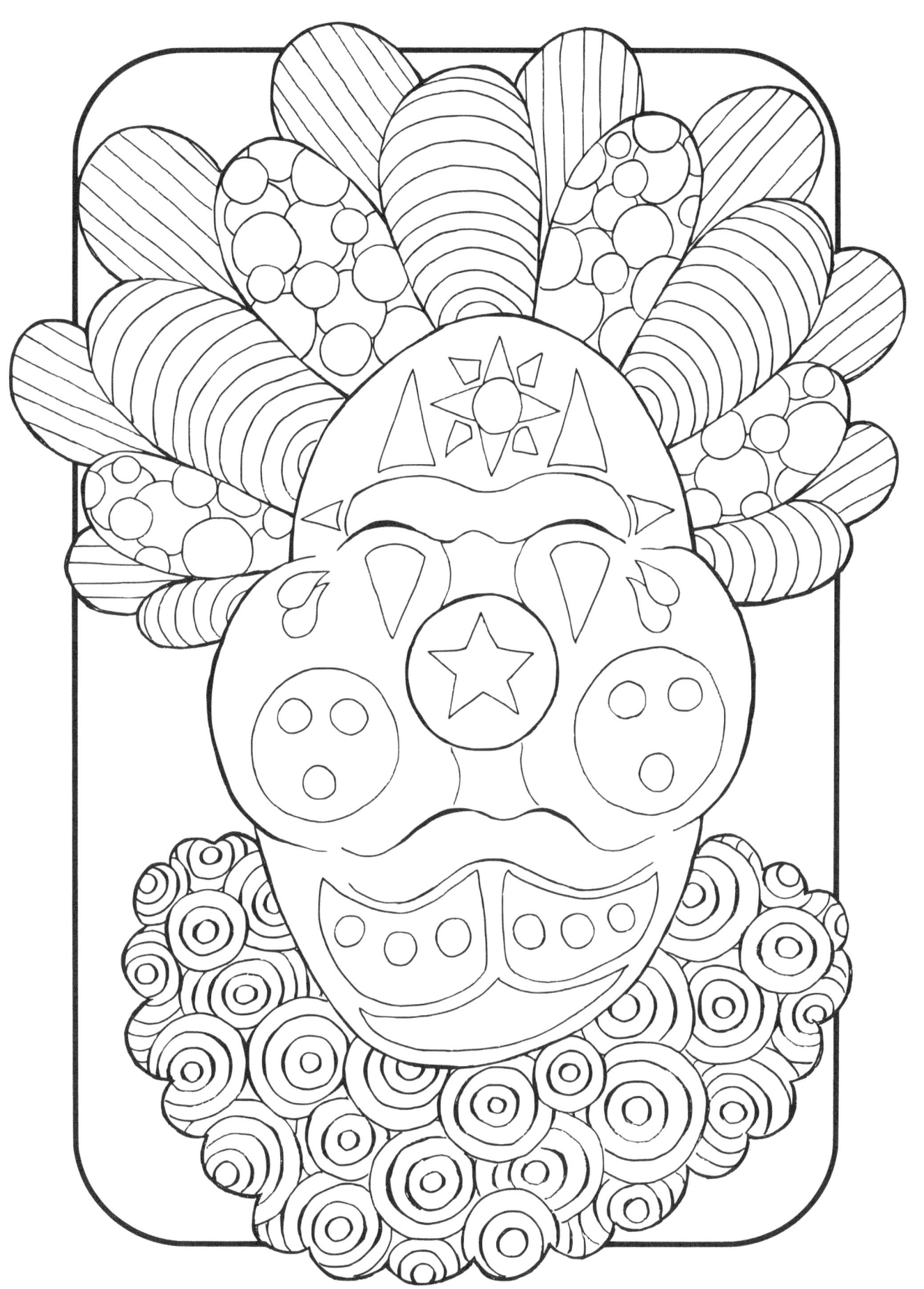

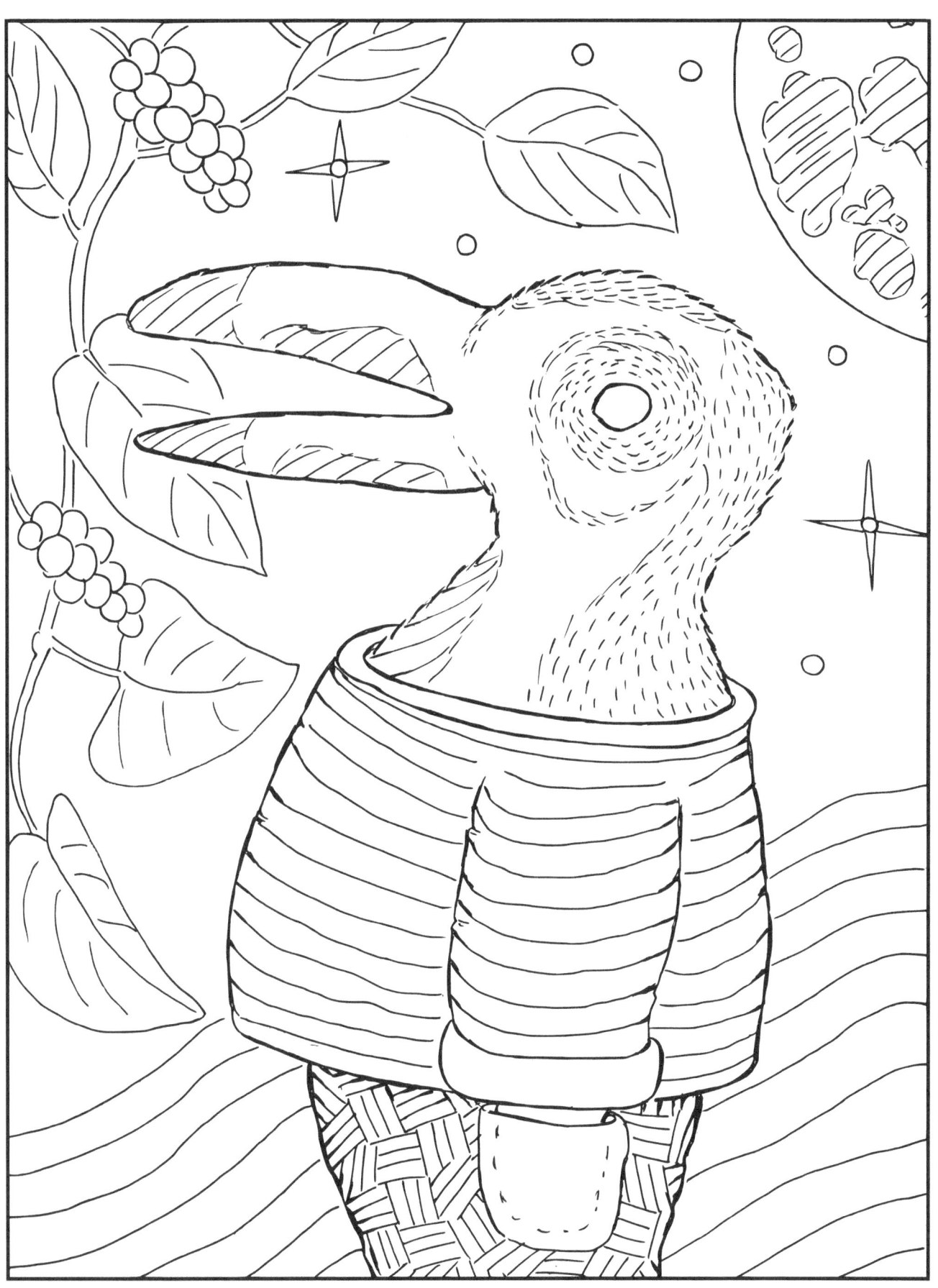

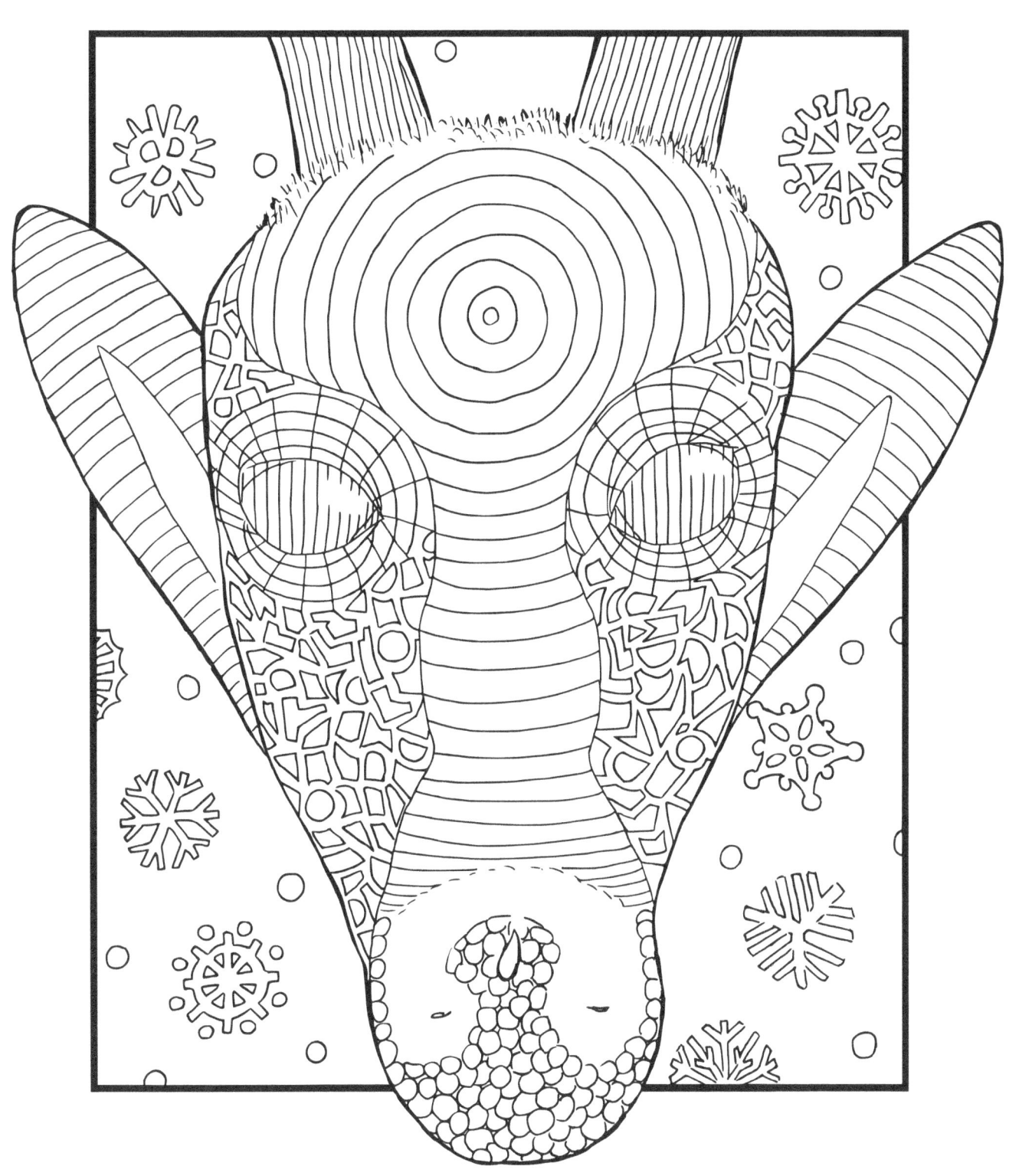

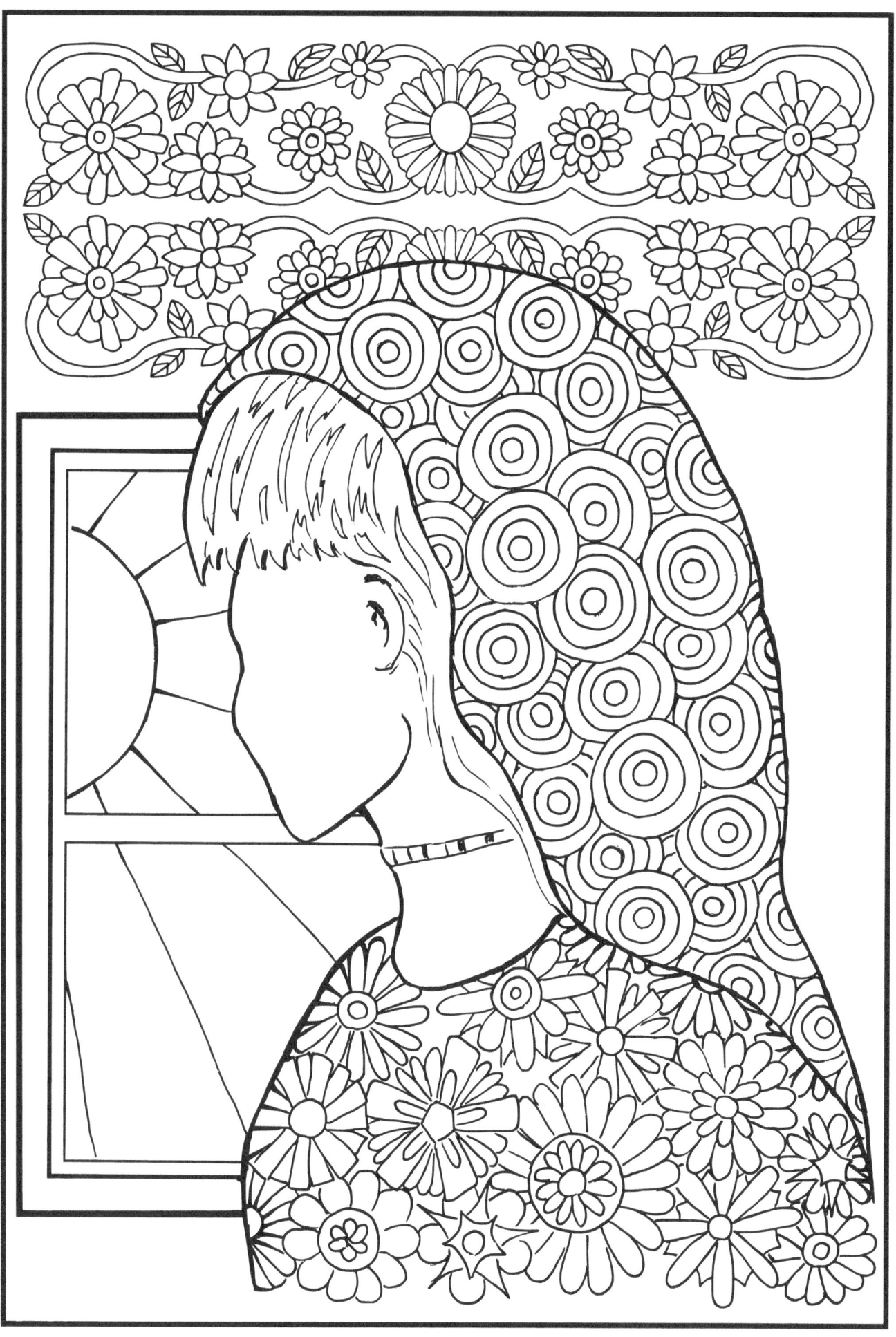

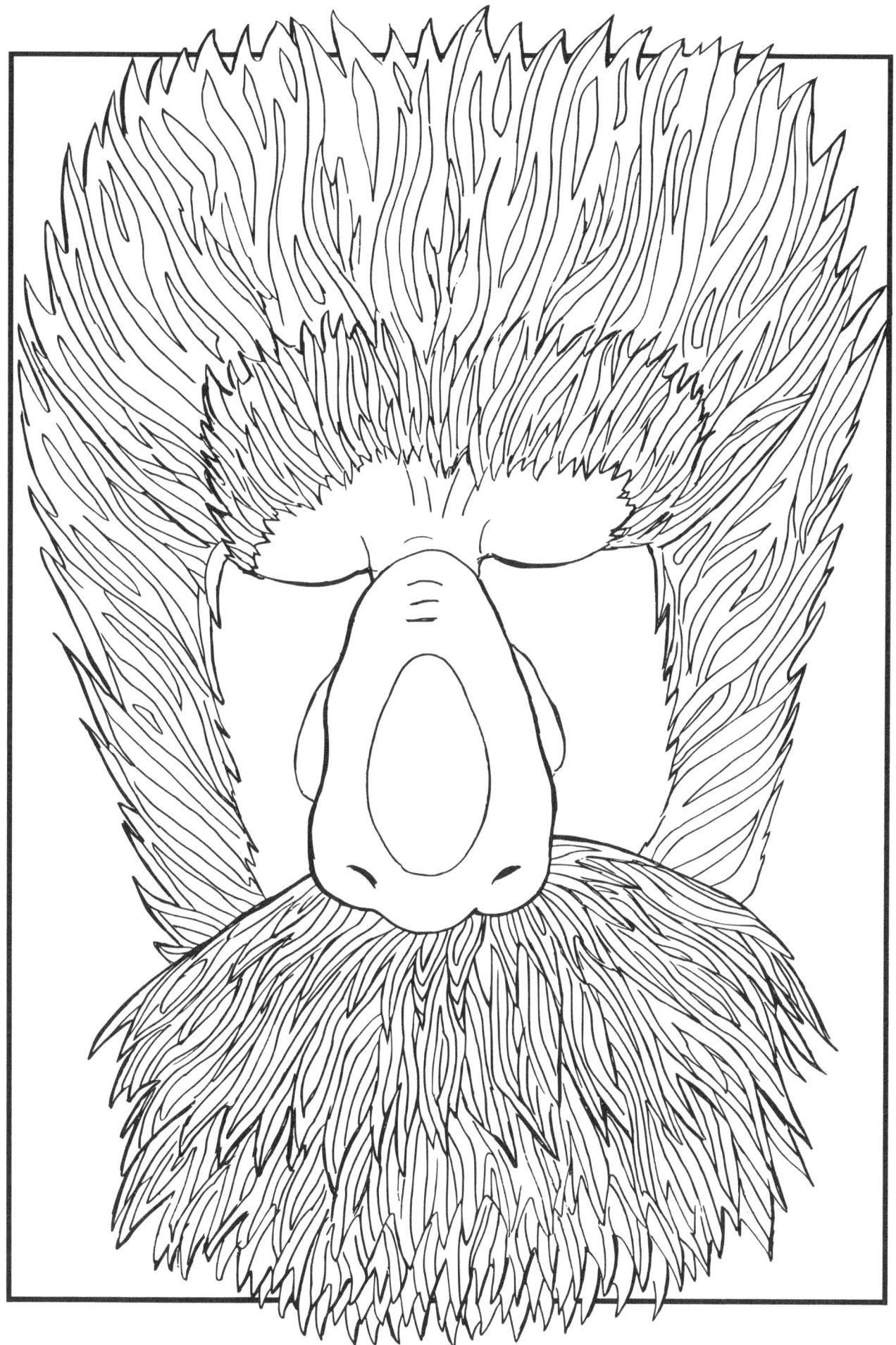

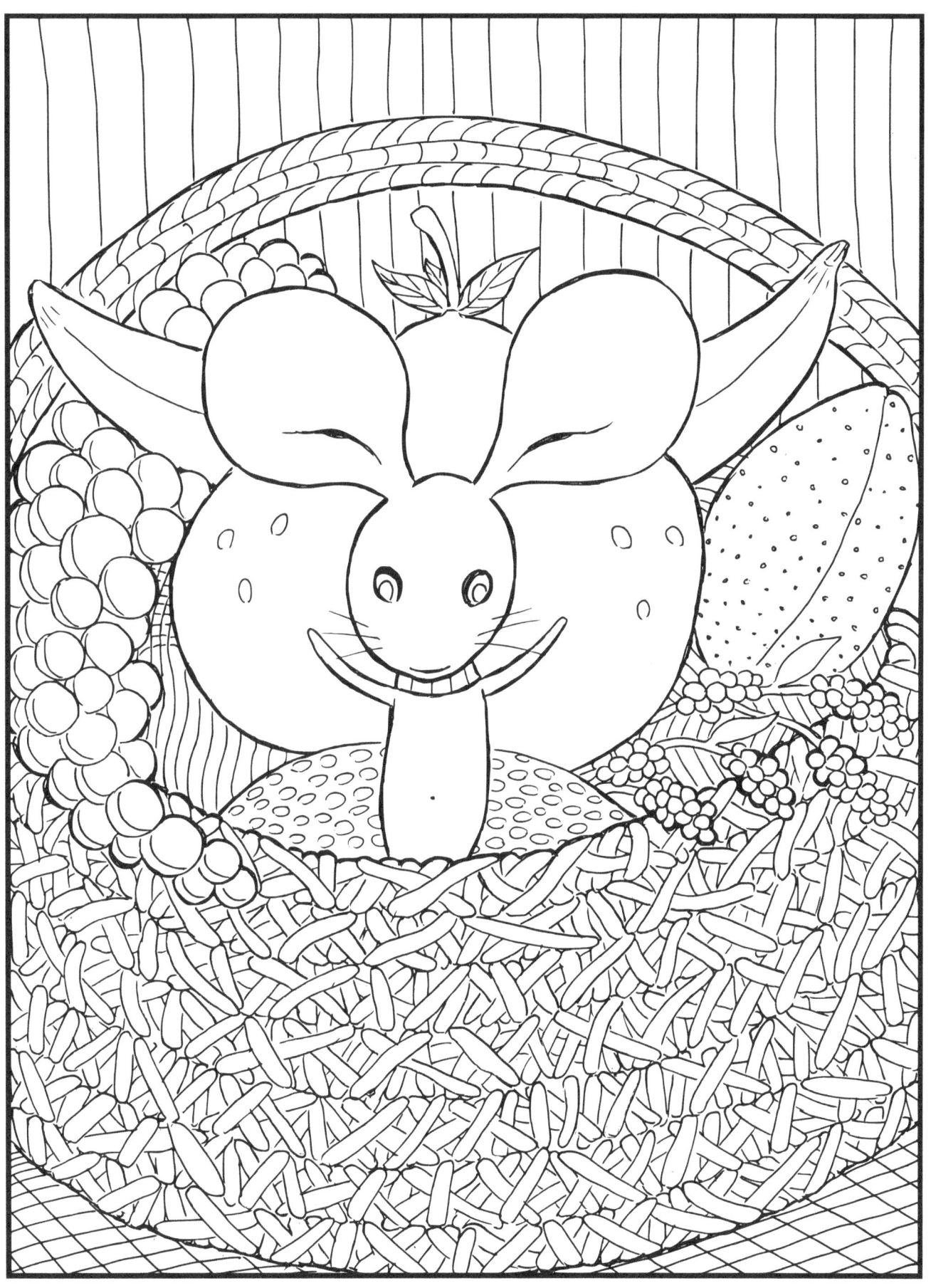

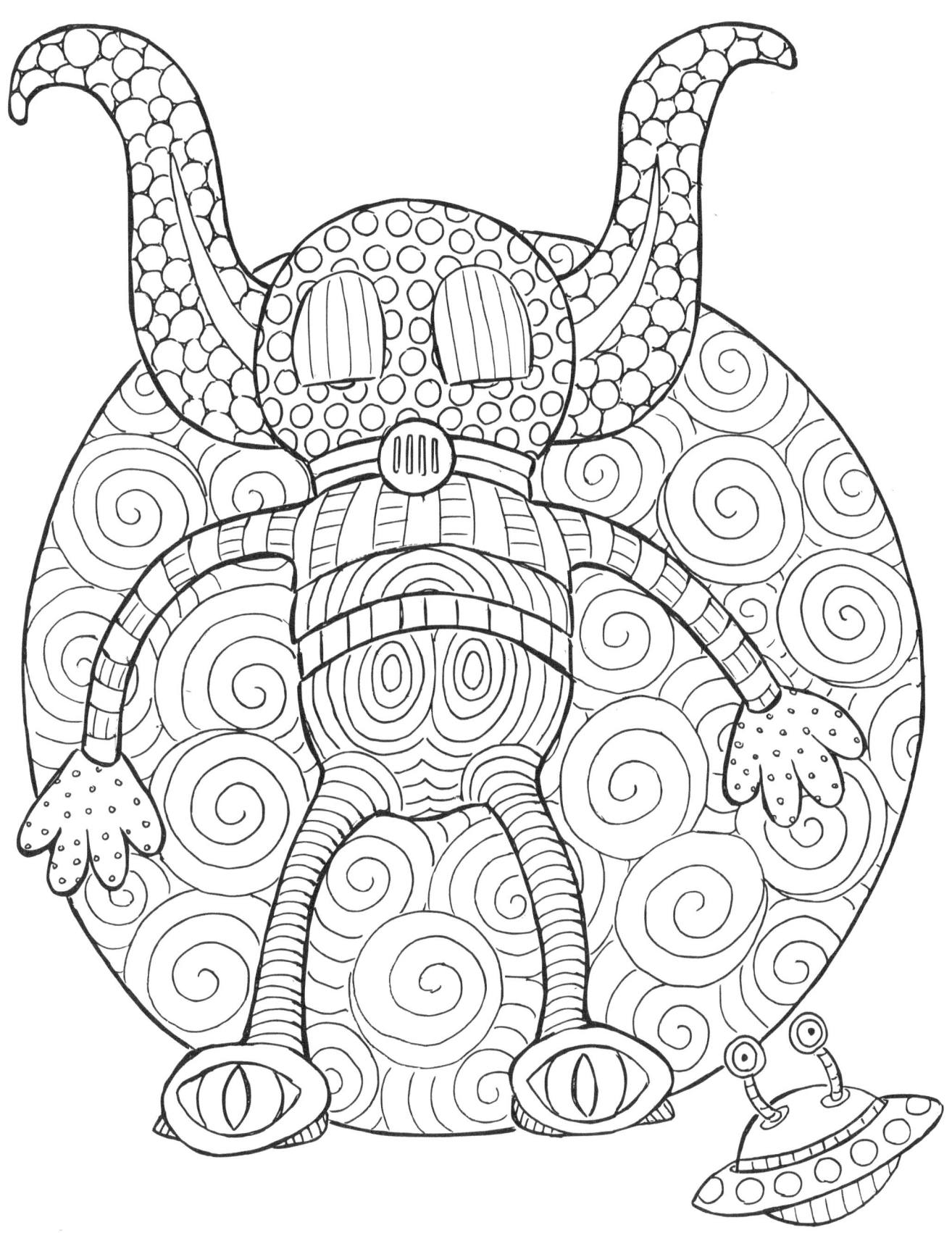

ANOTHER TRY!
(Duplicate Coloring Pages)

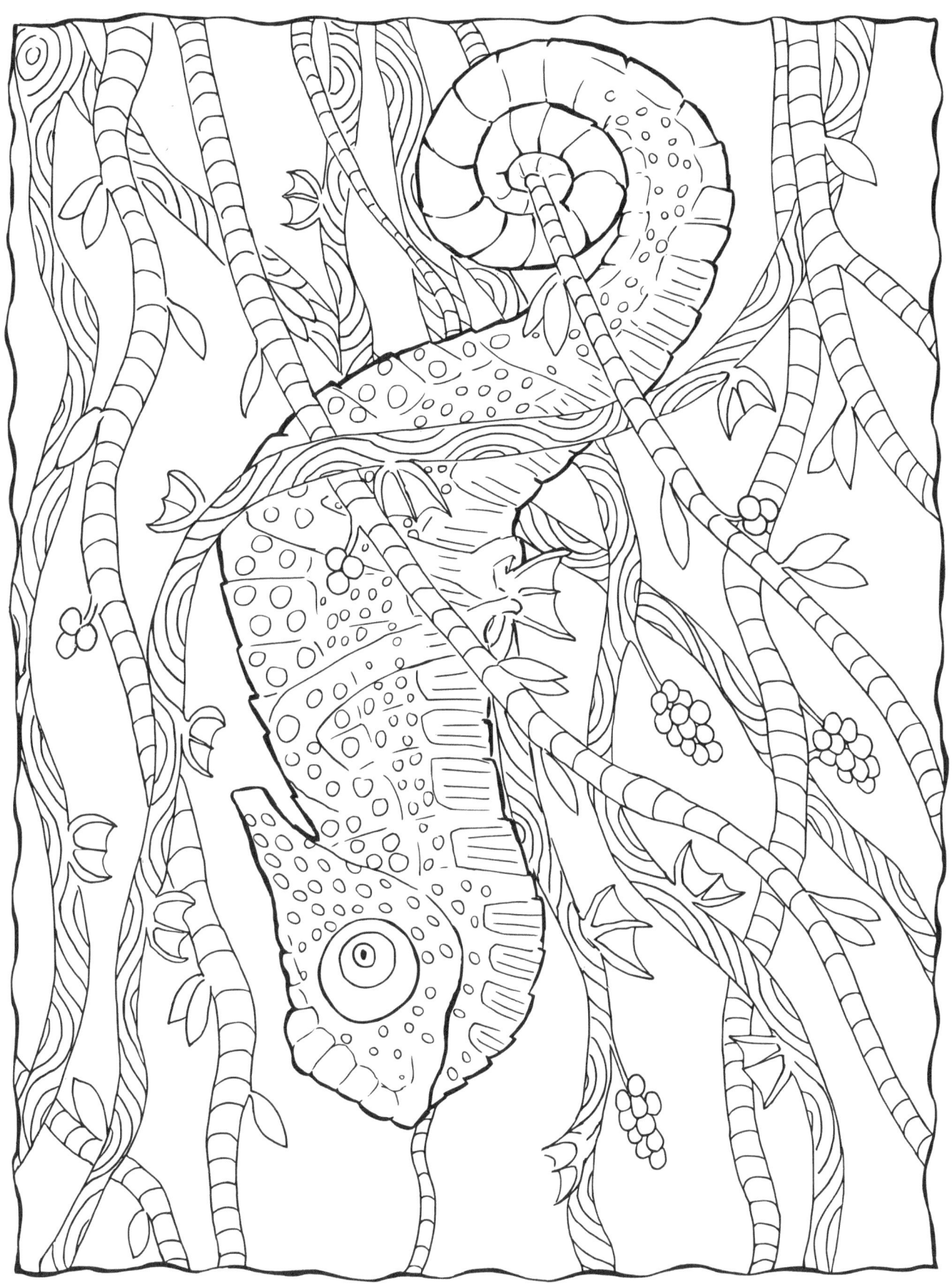

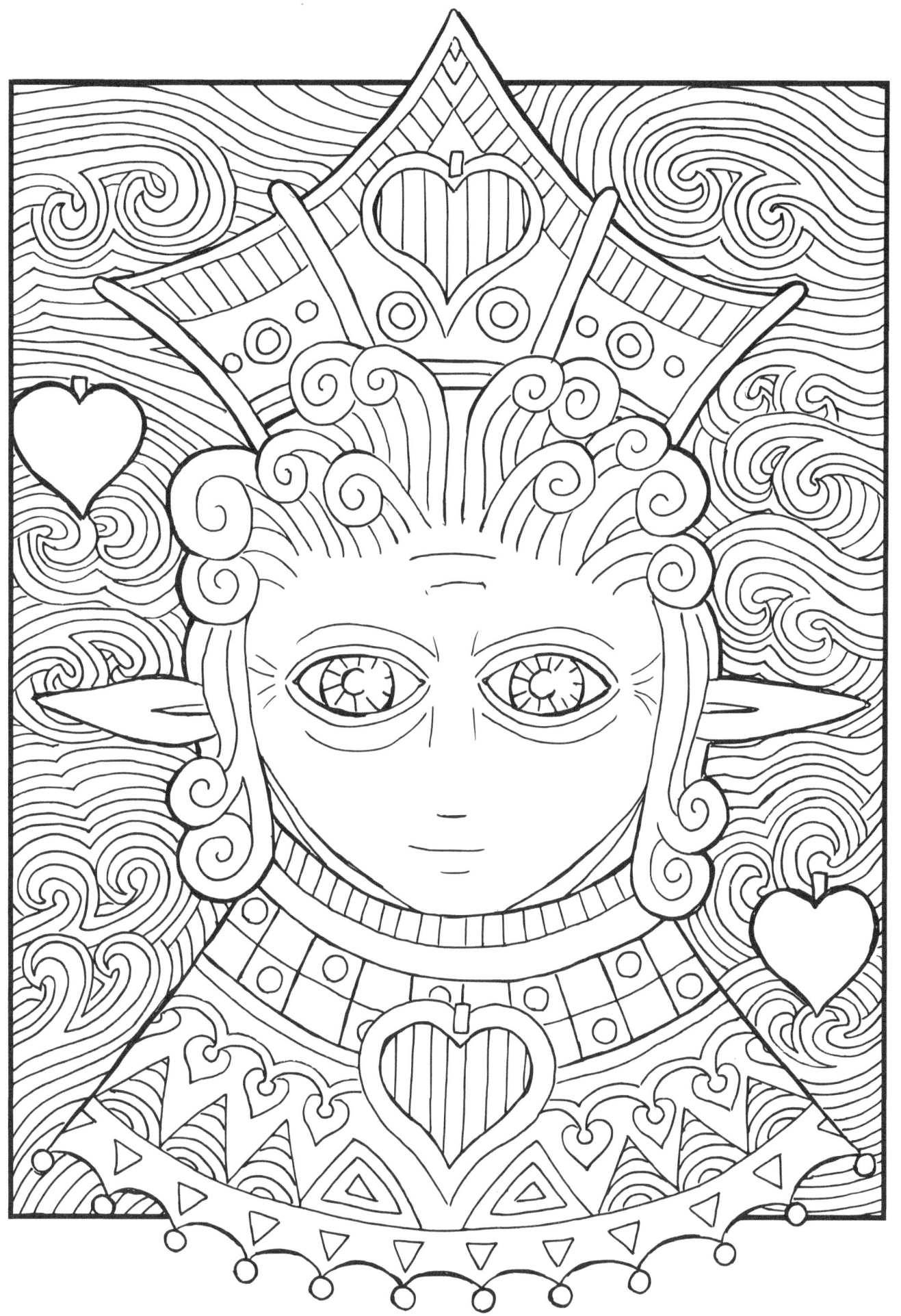

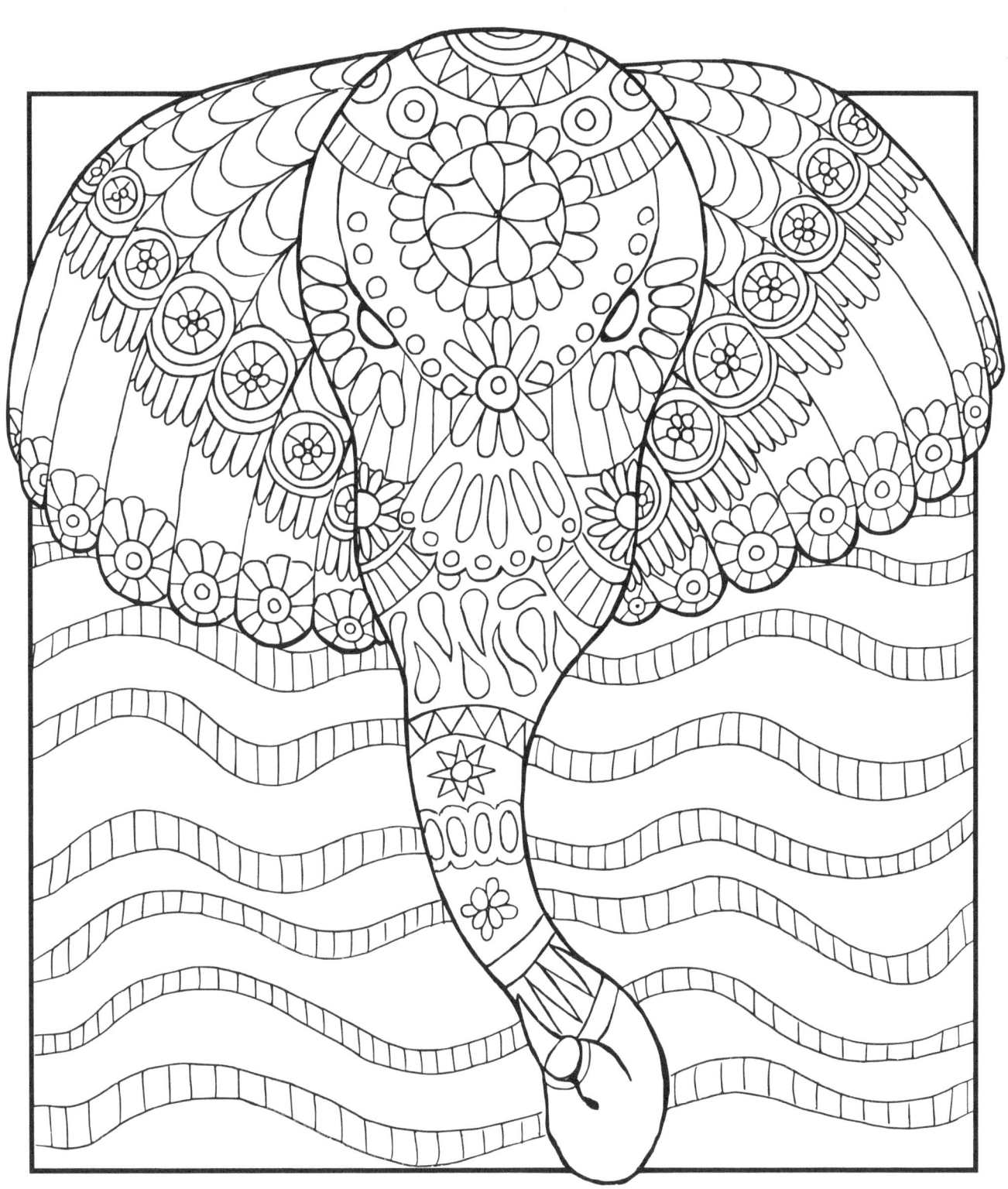

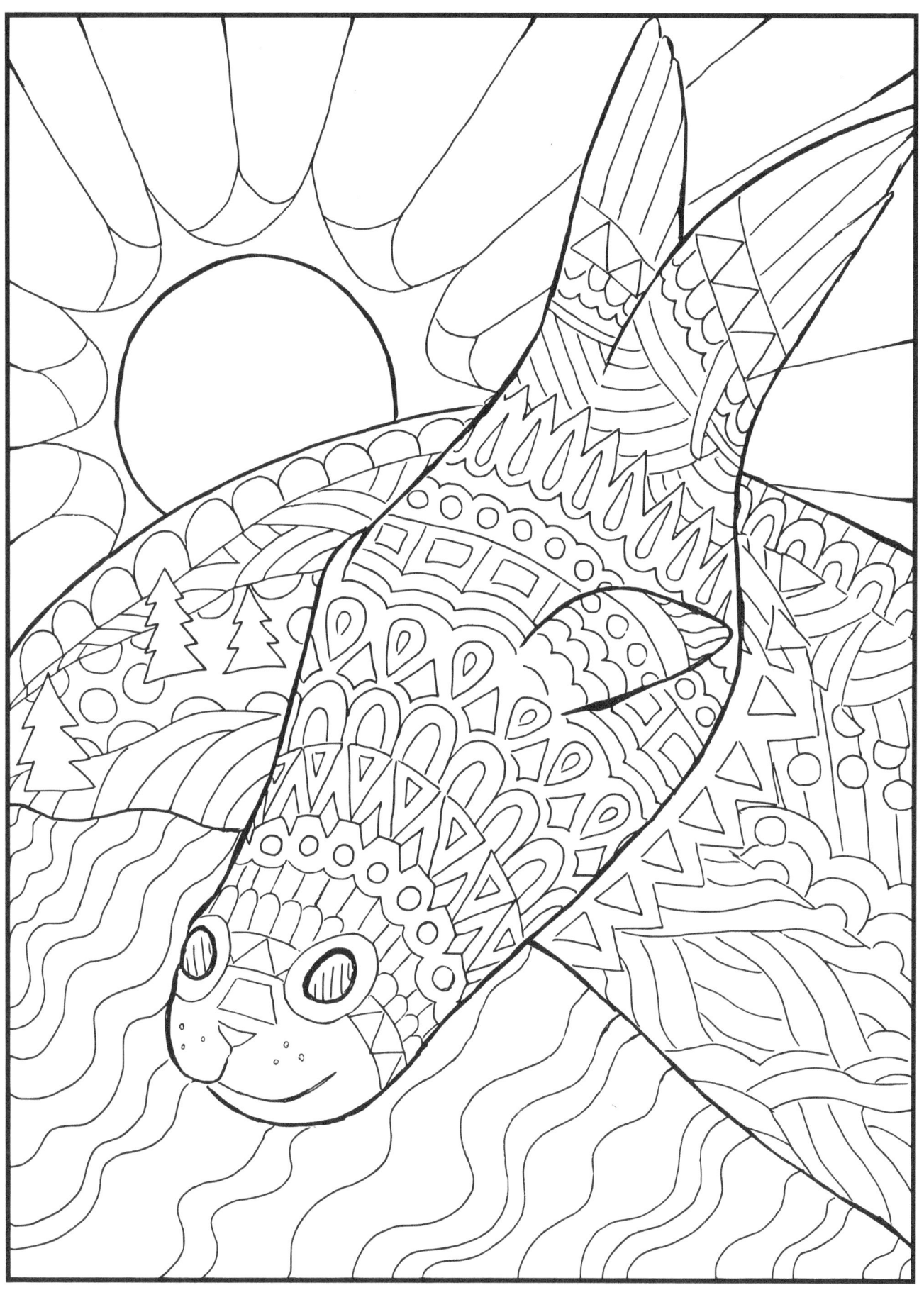

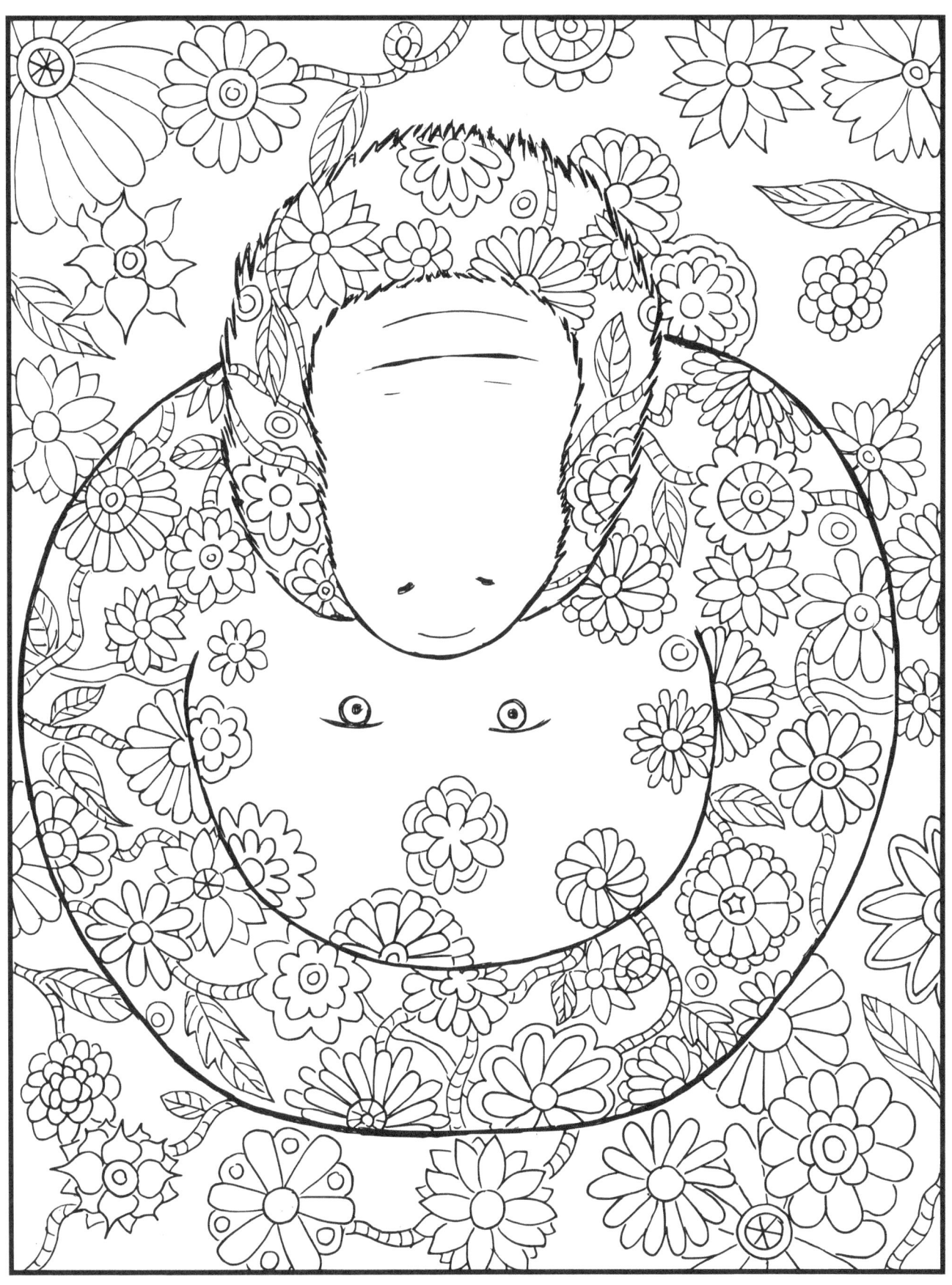

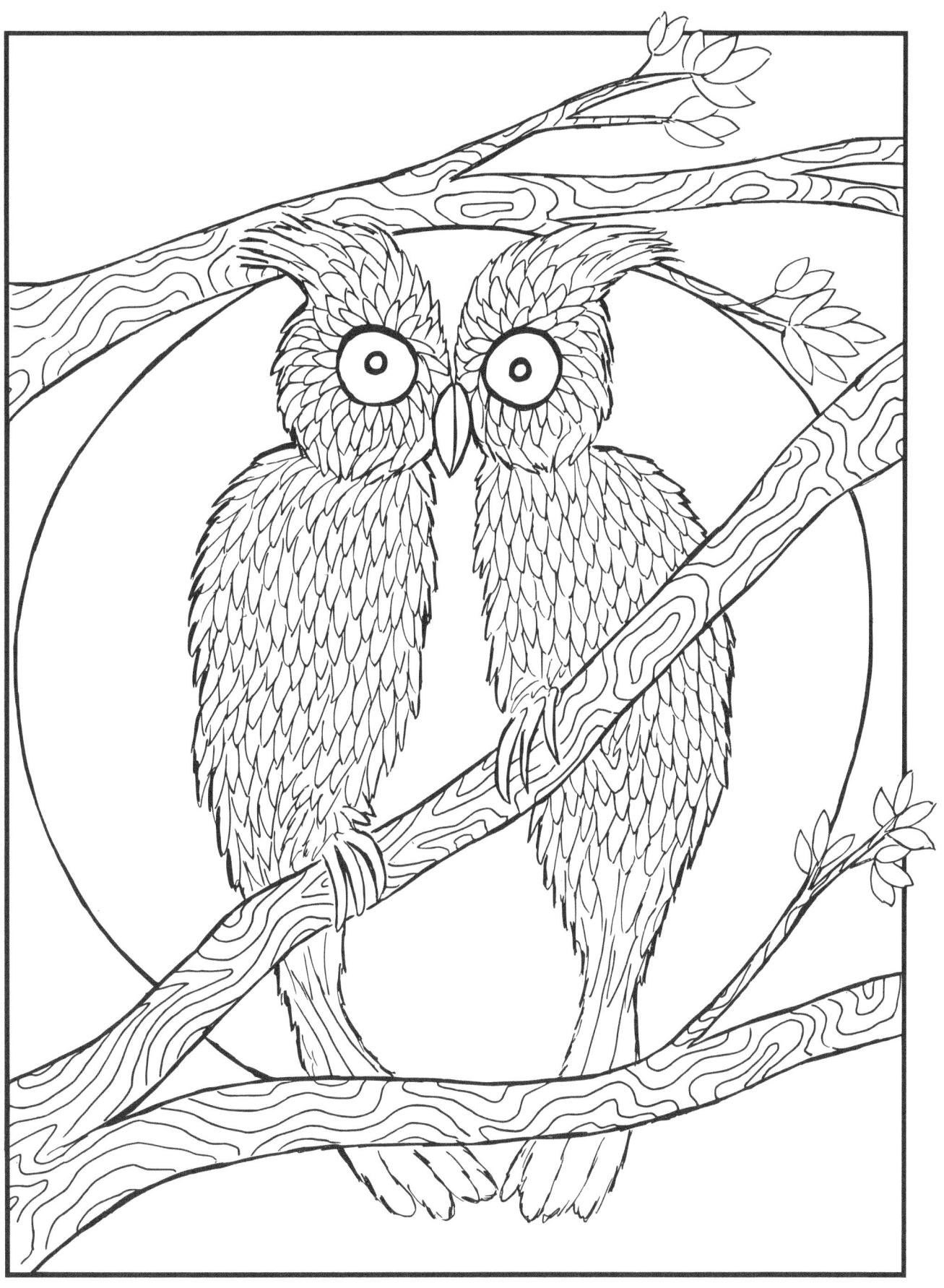

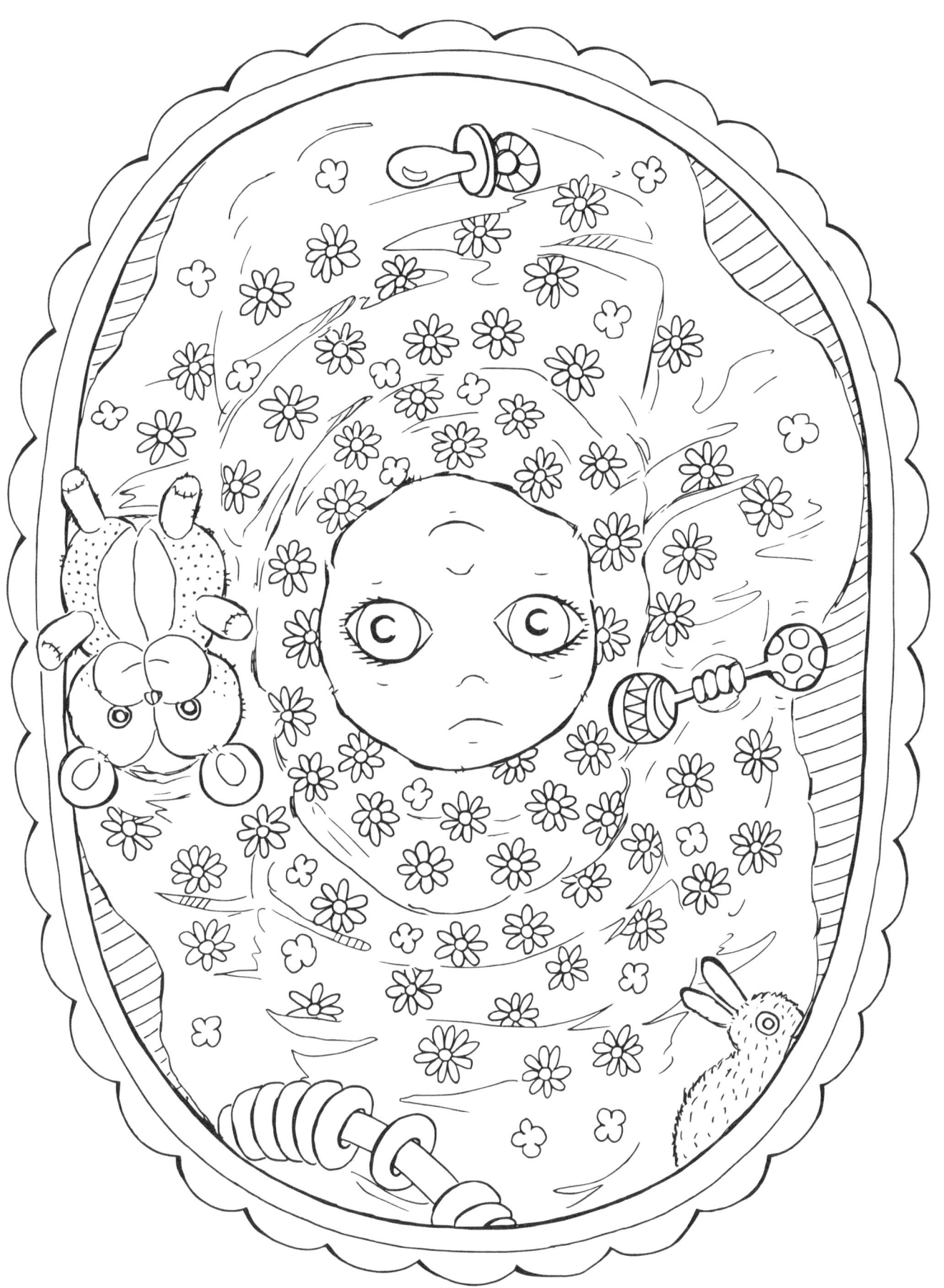

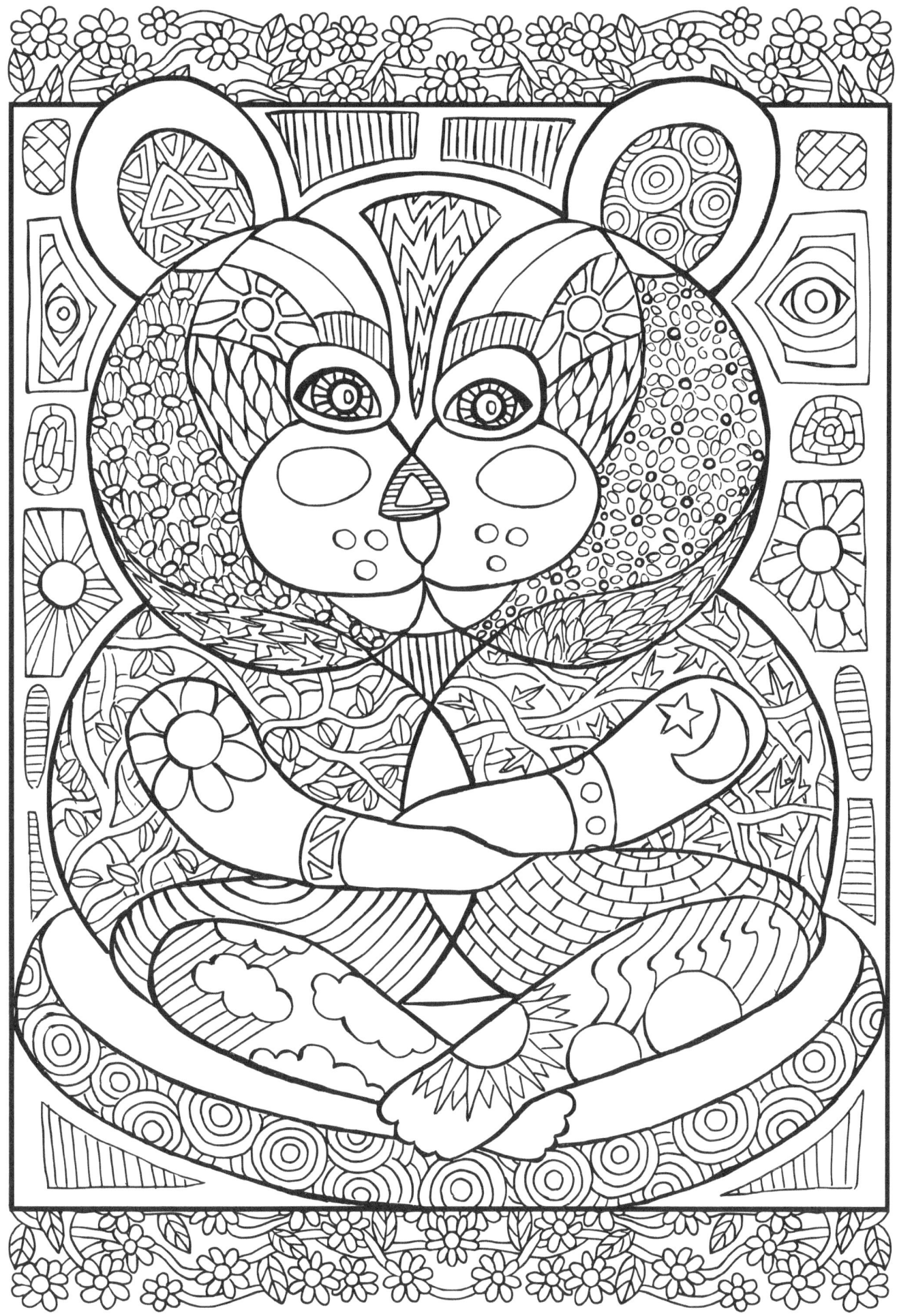

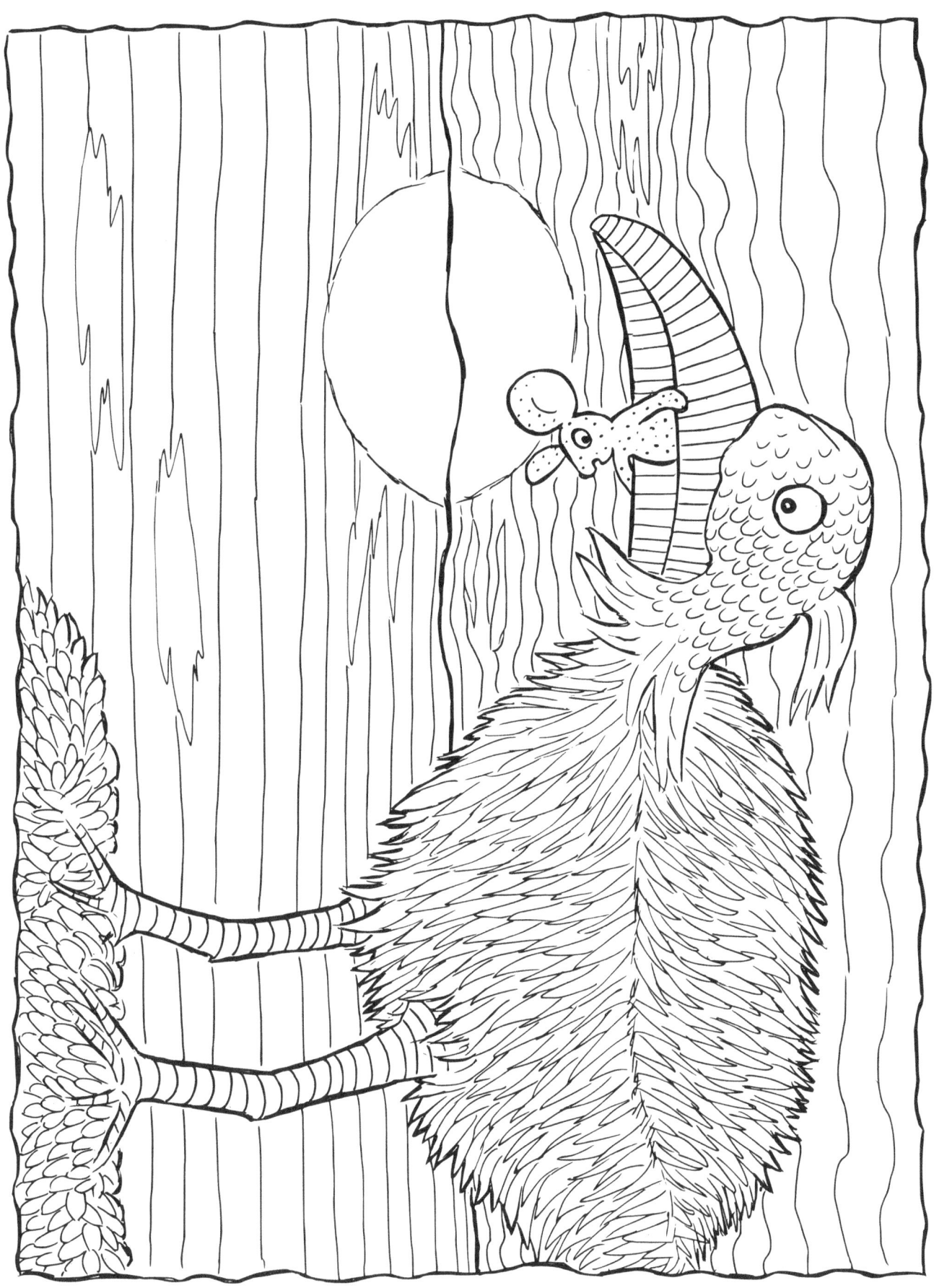

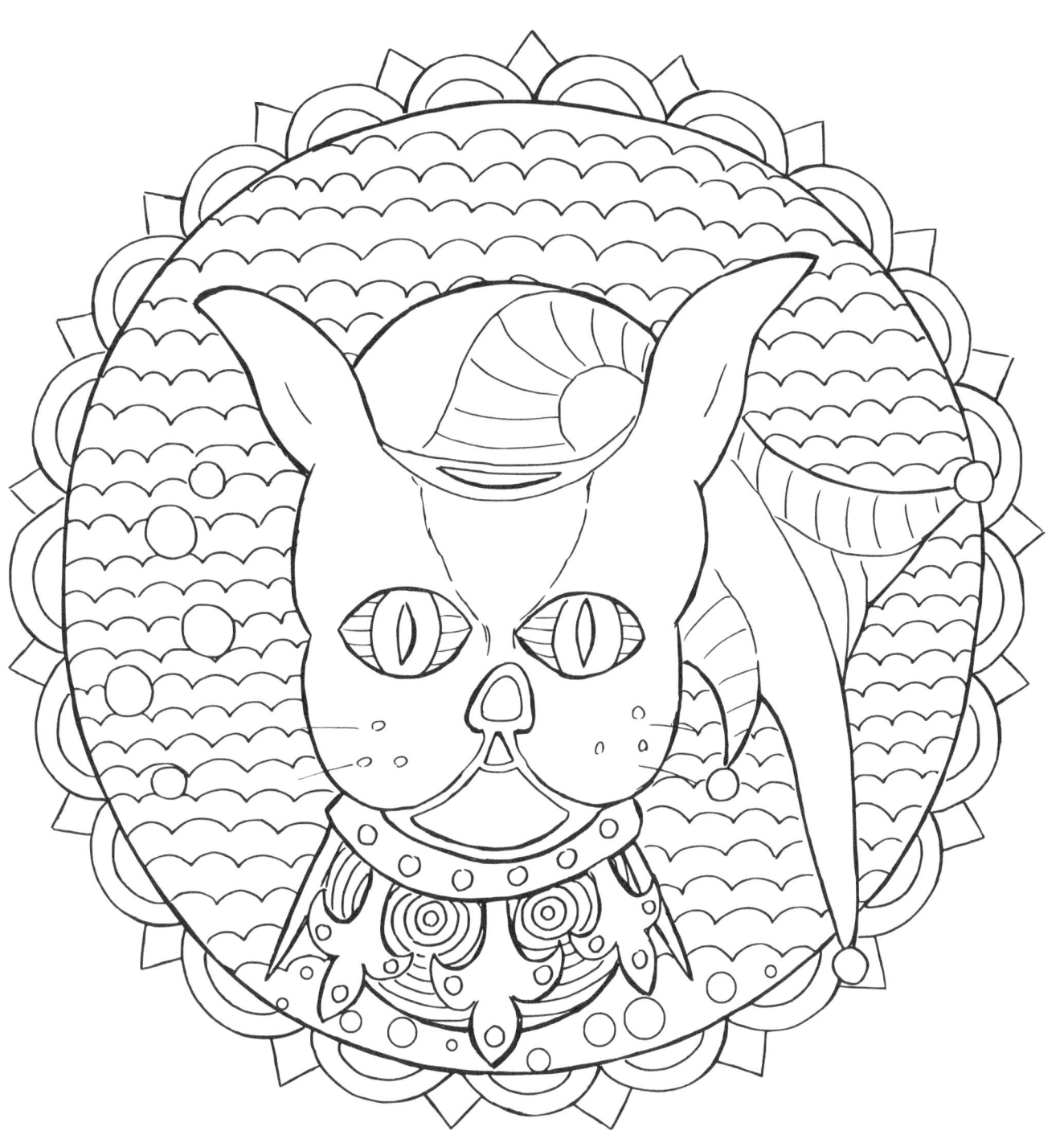

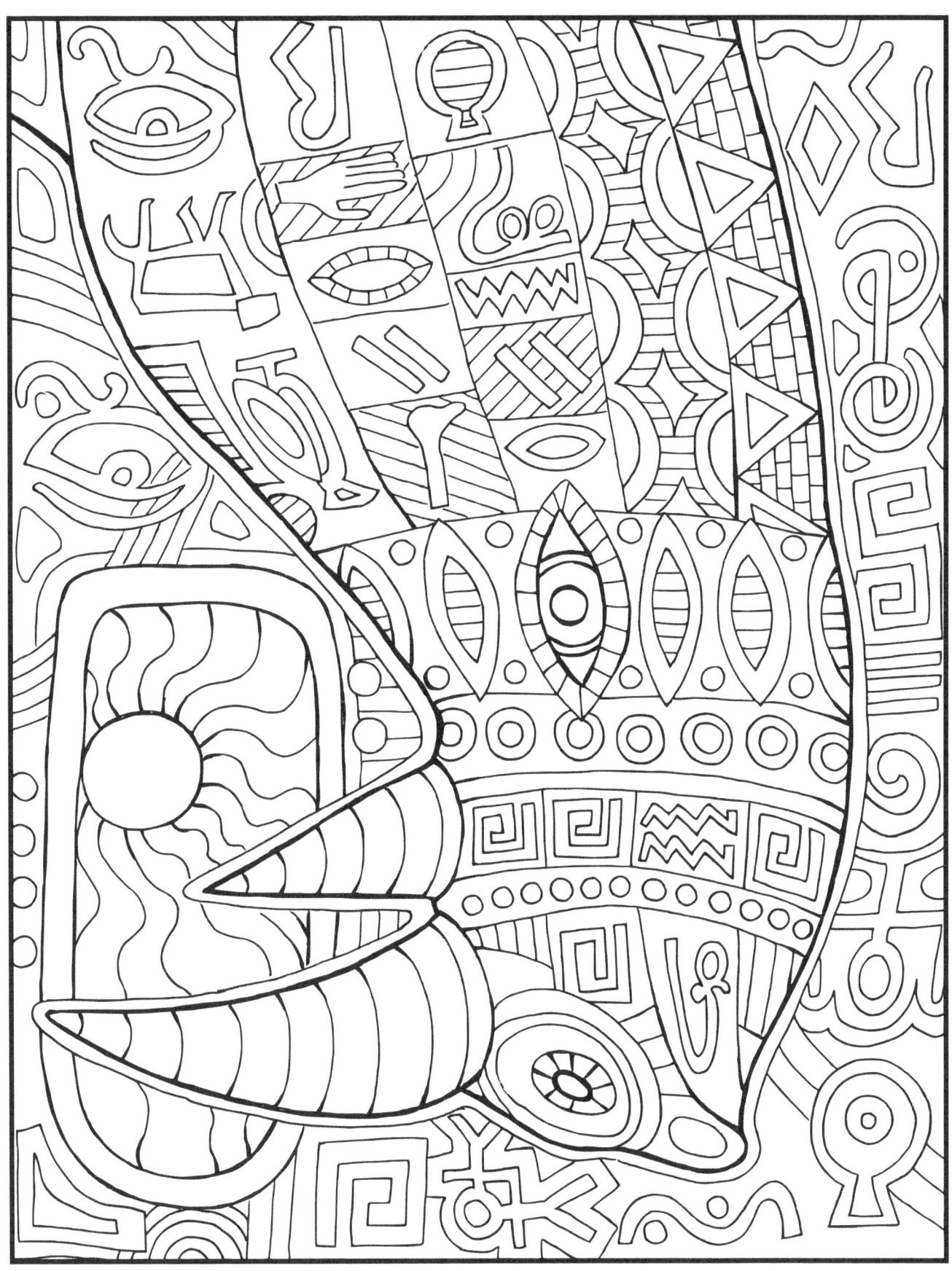

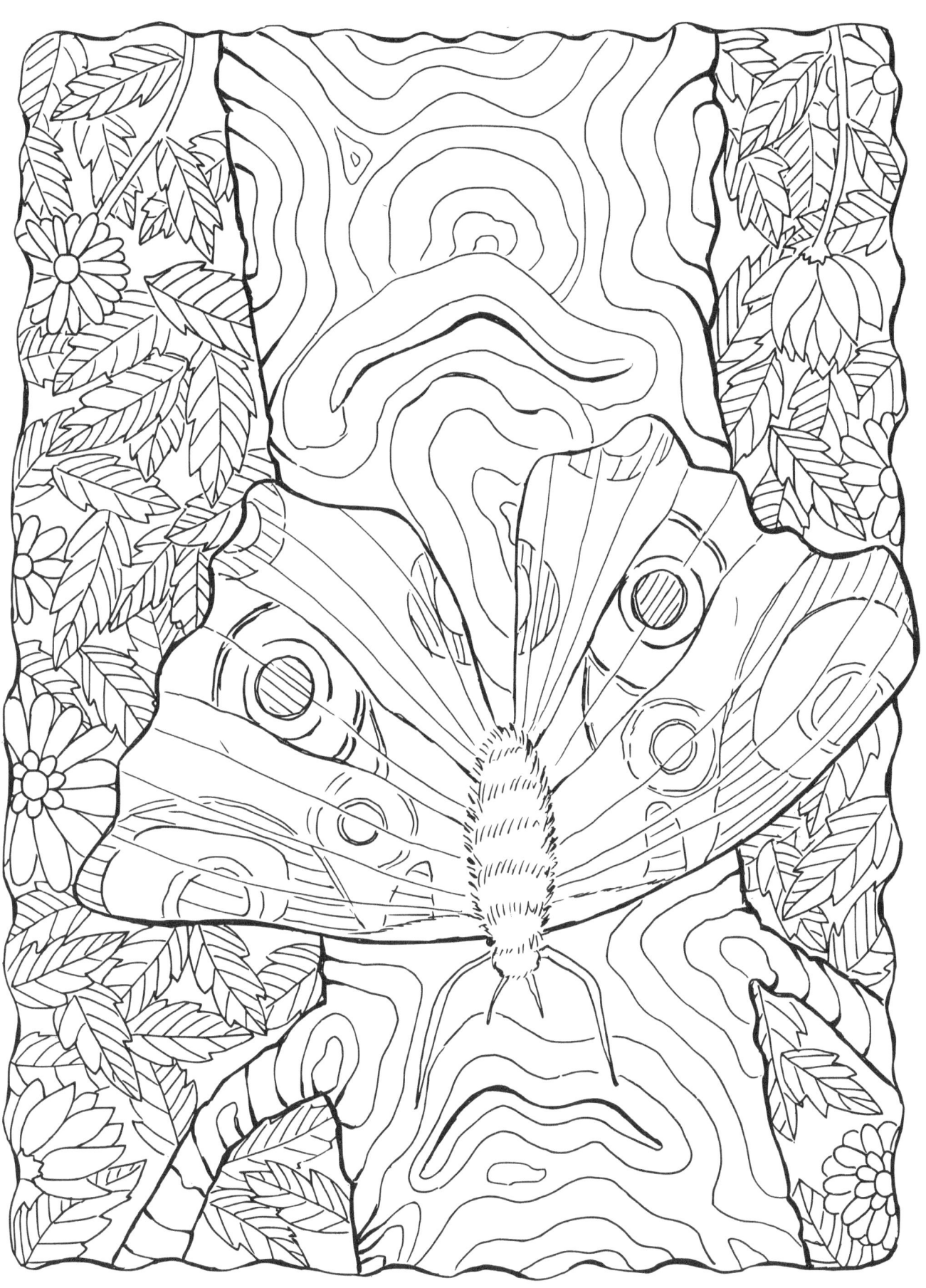

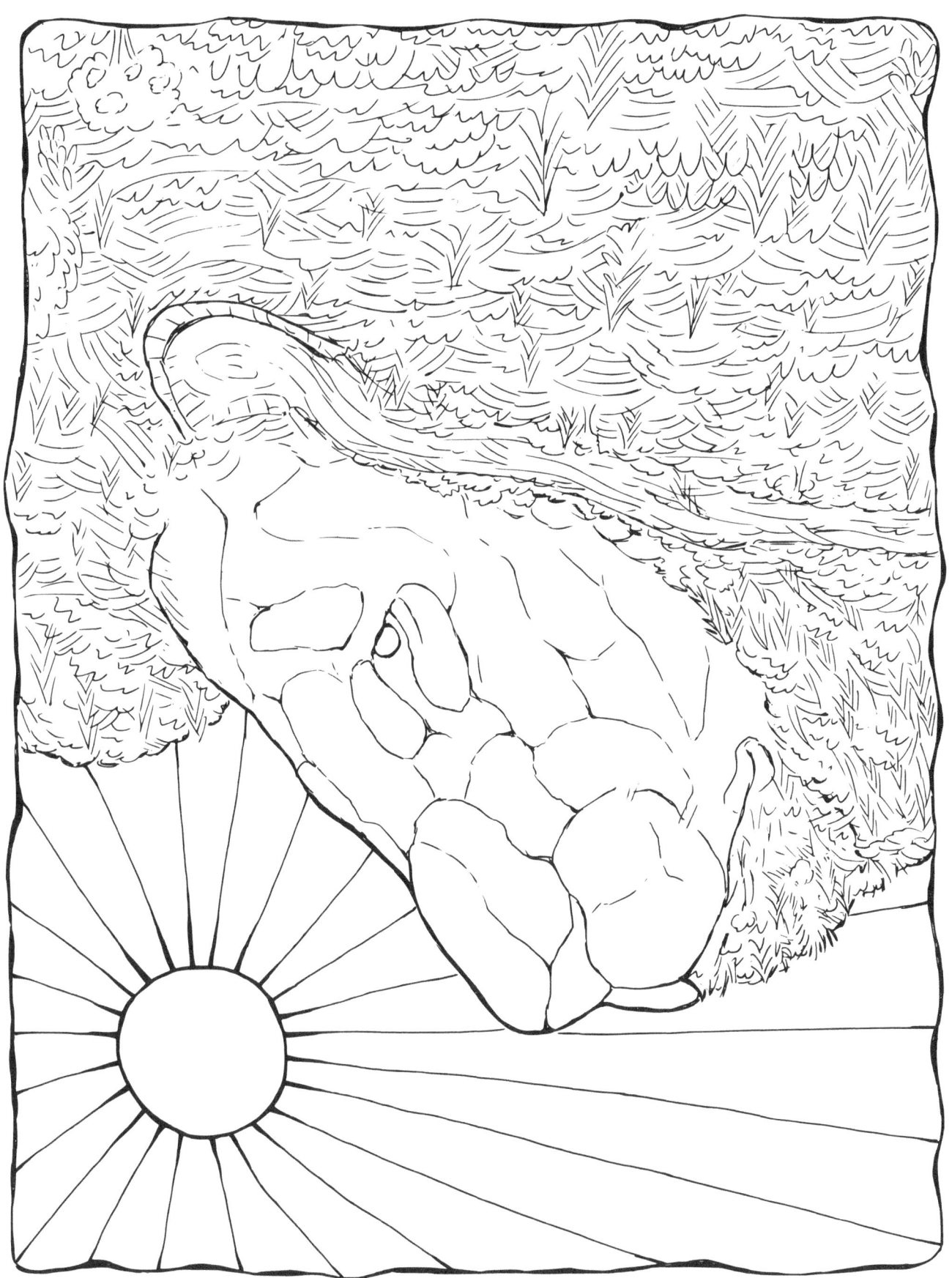

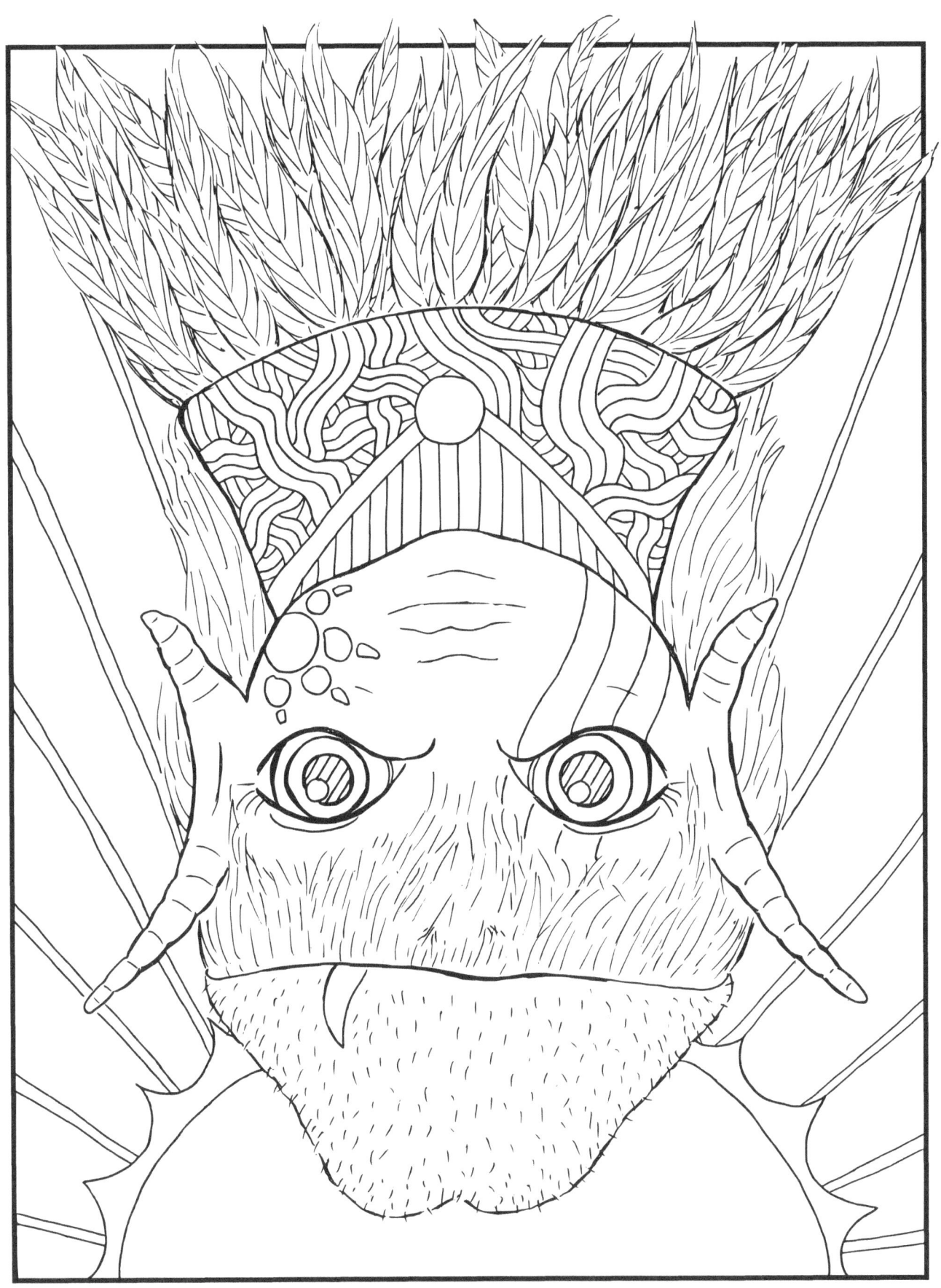

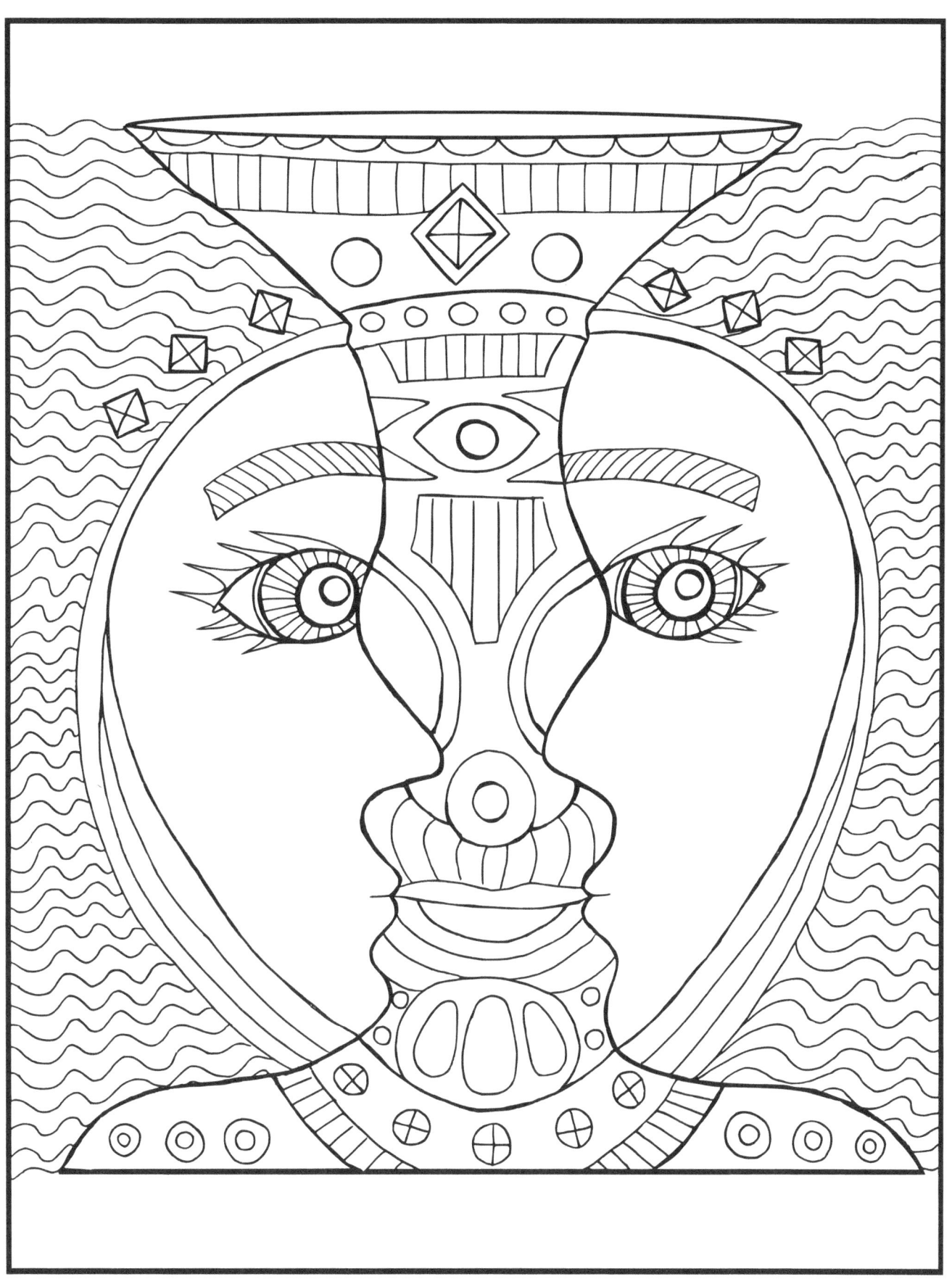

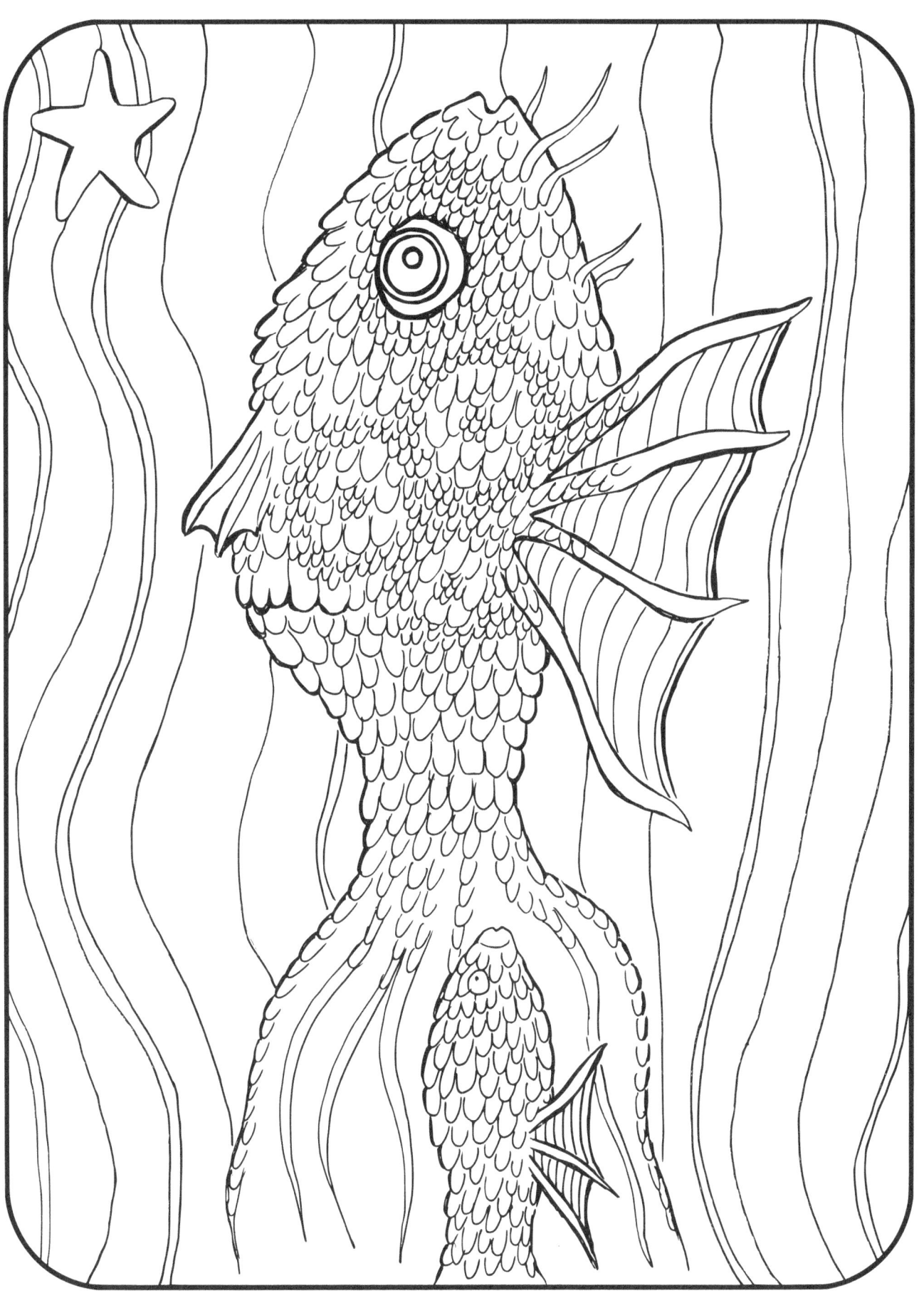

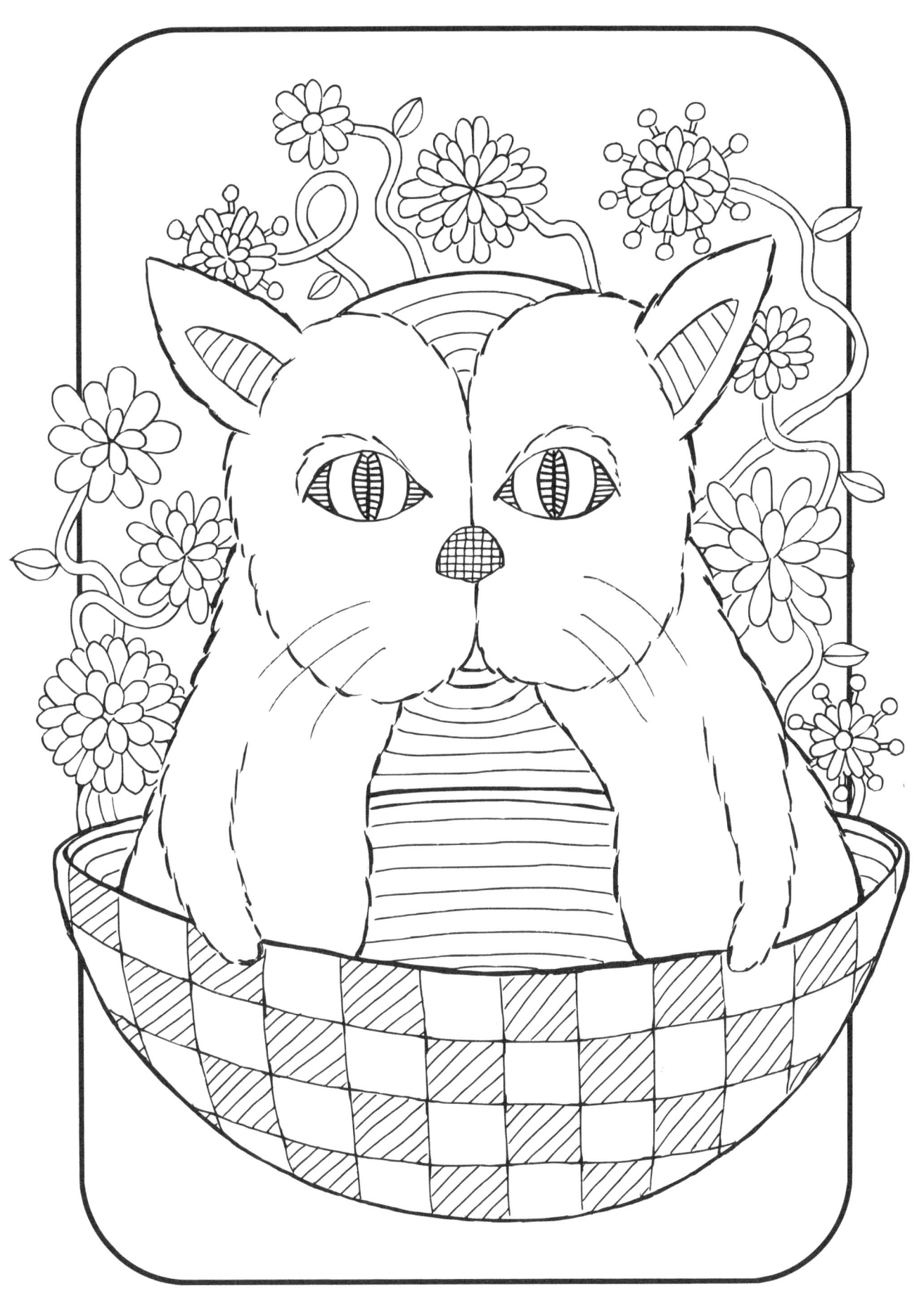

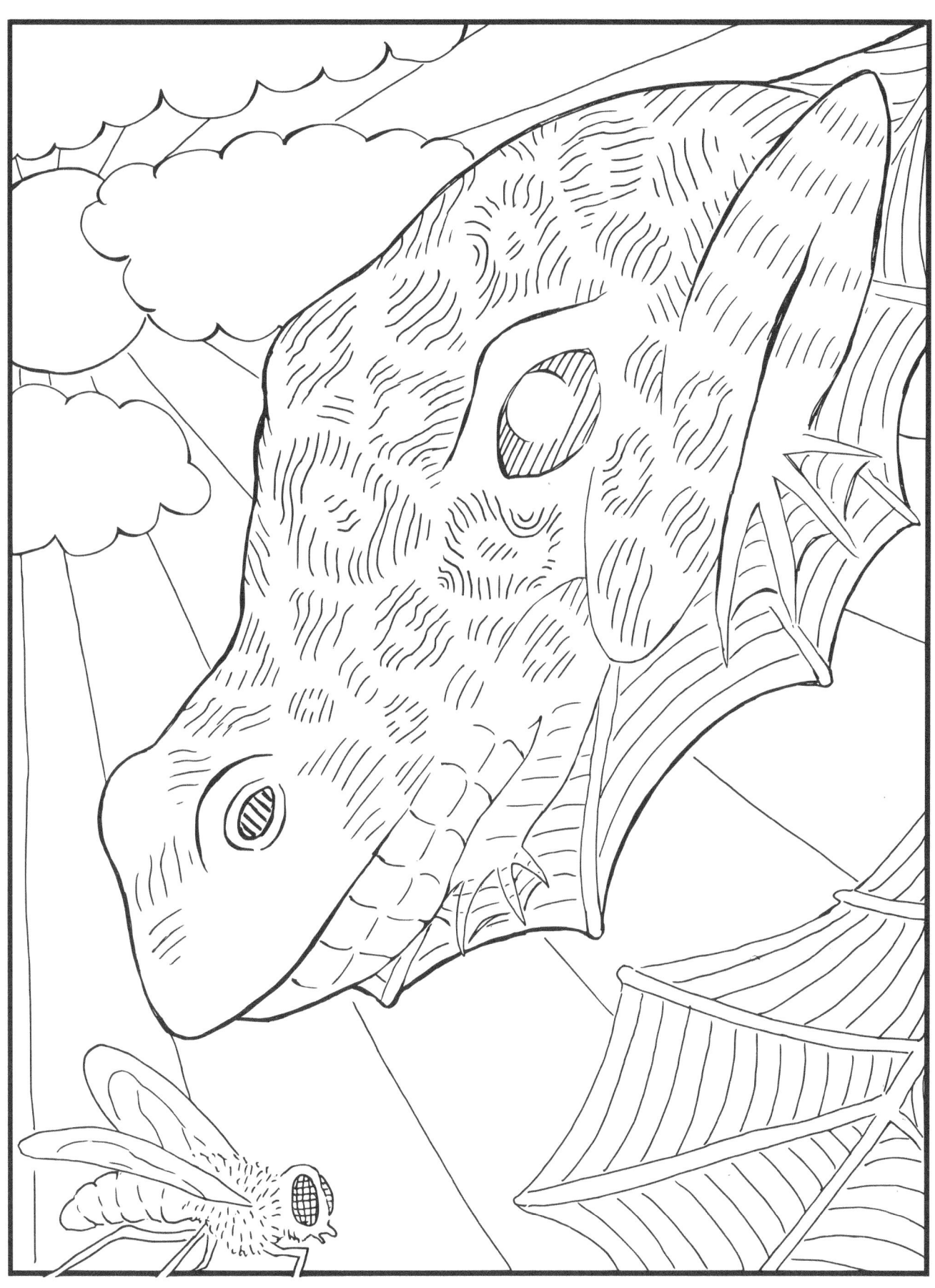

.

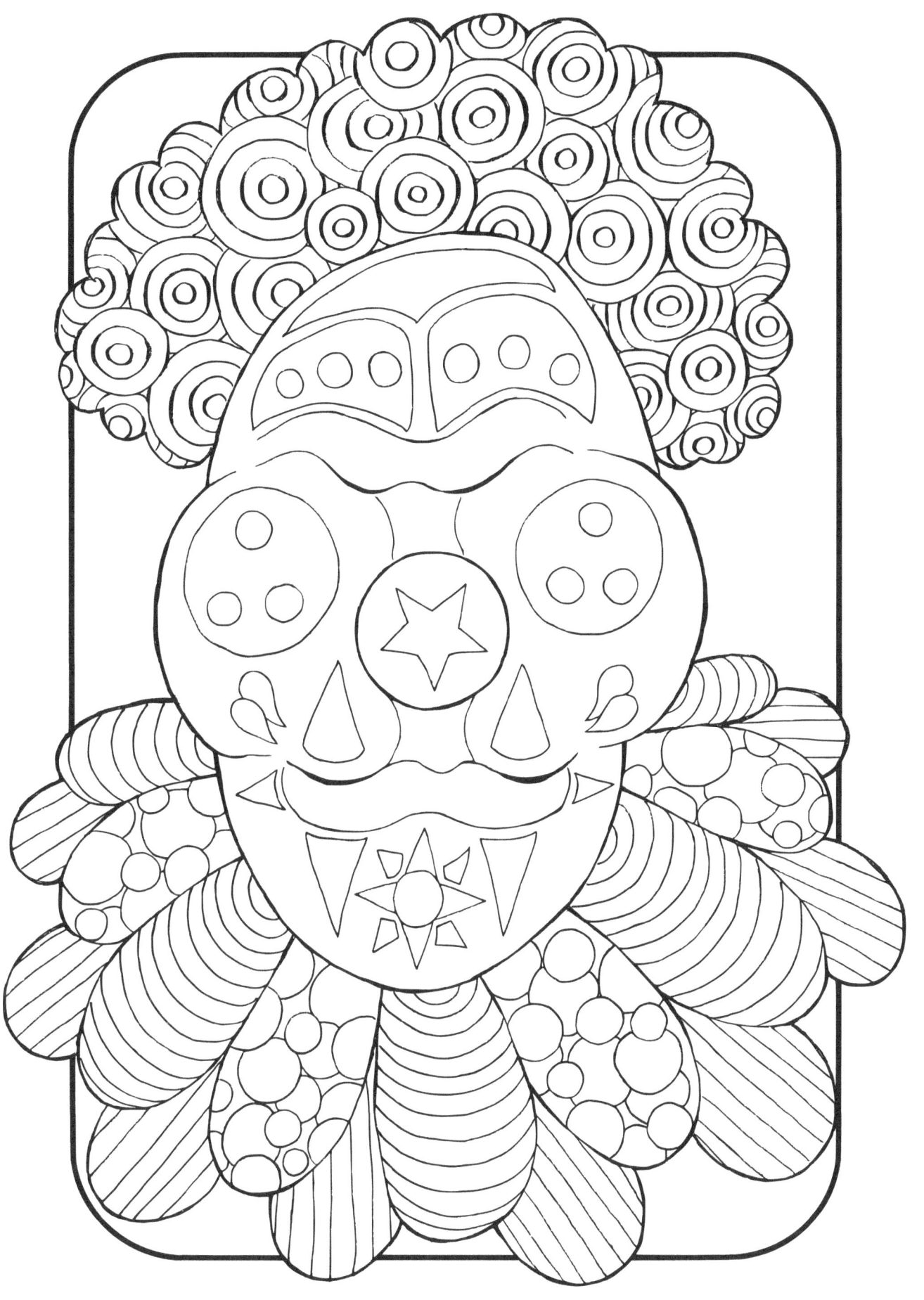

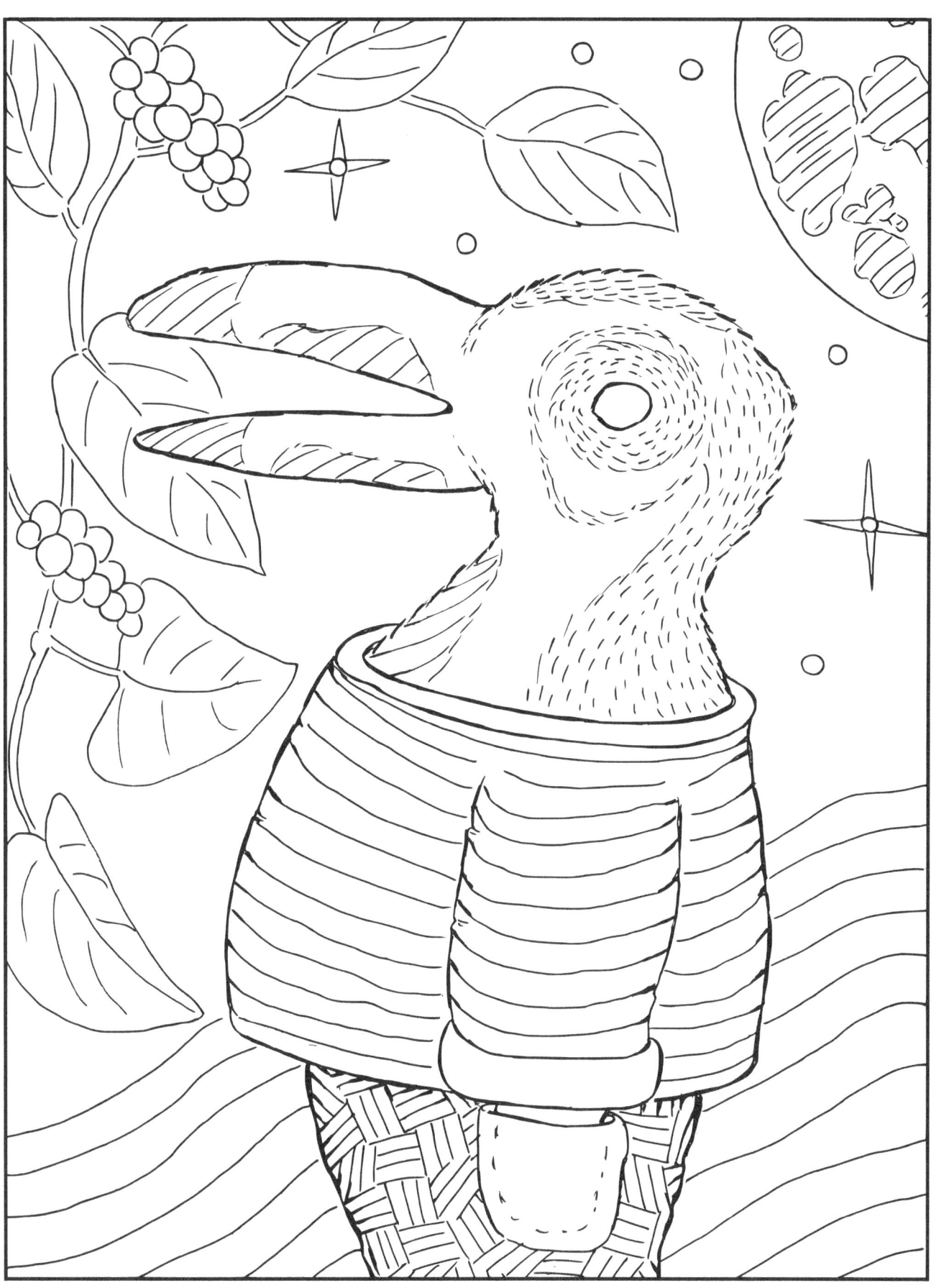

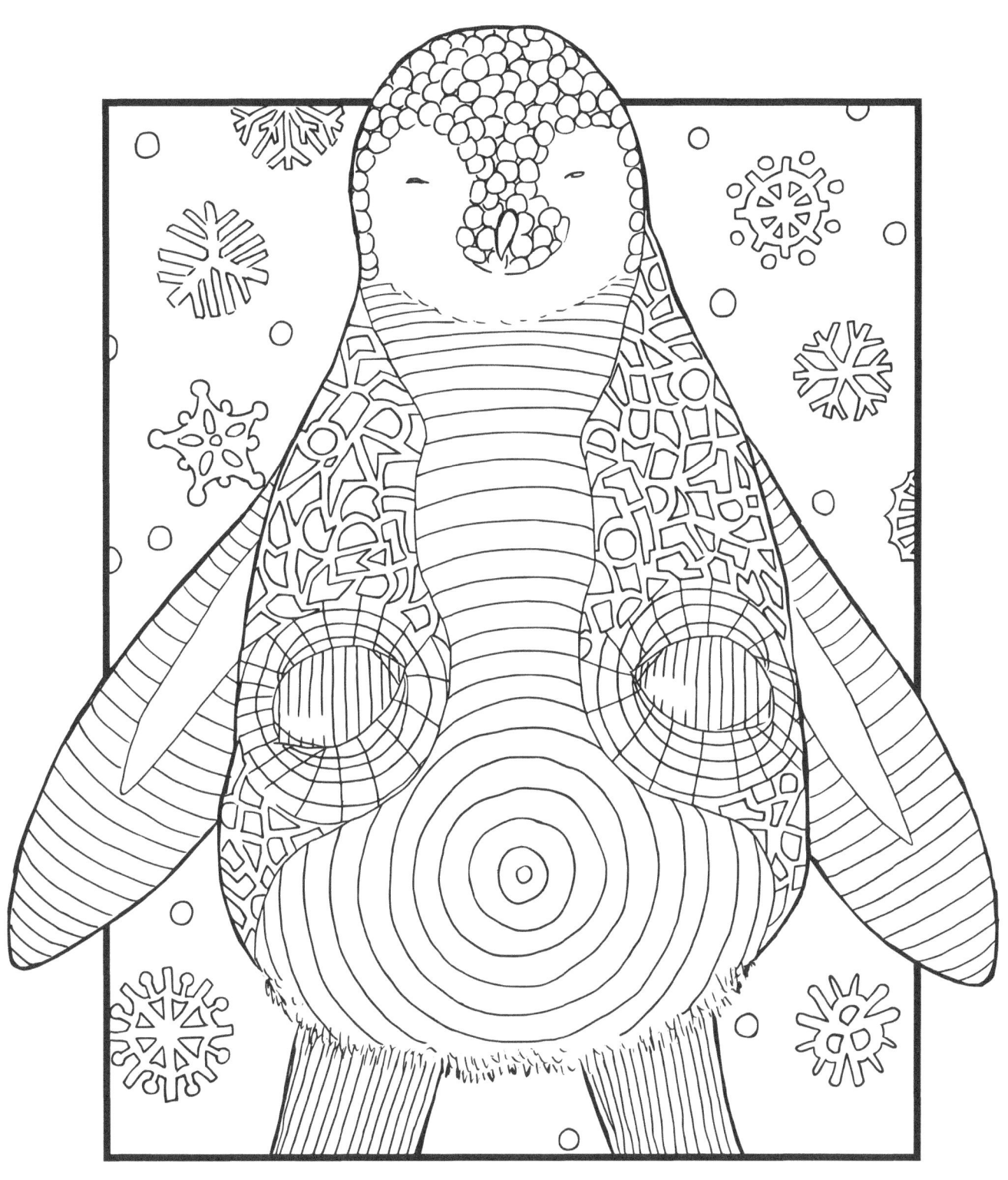

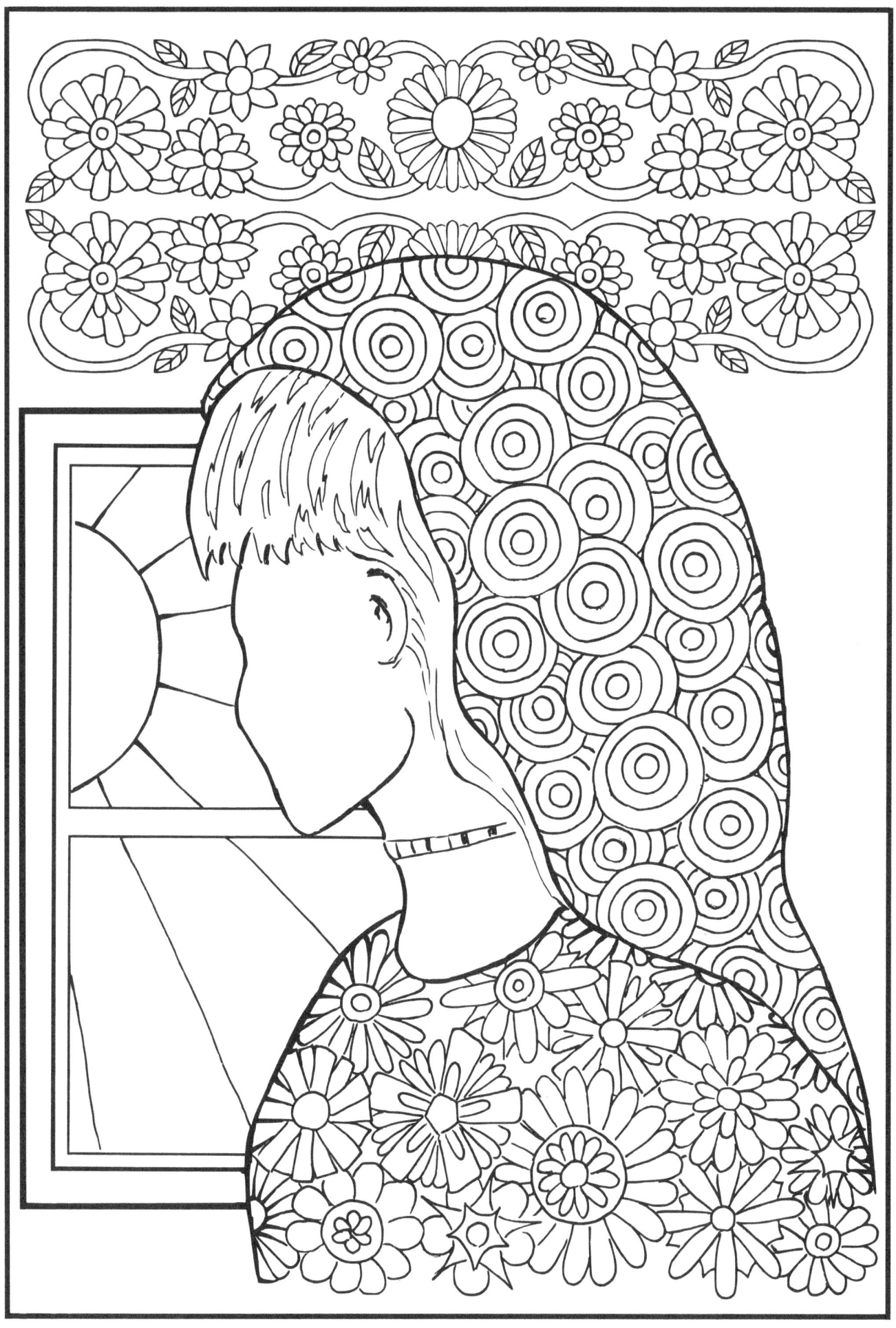

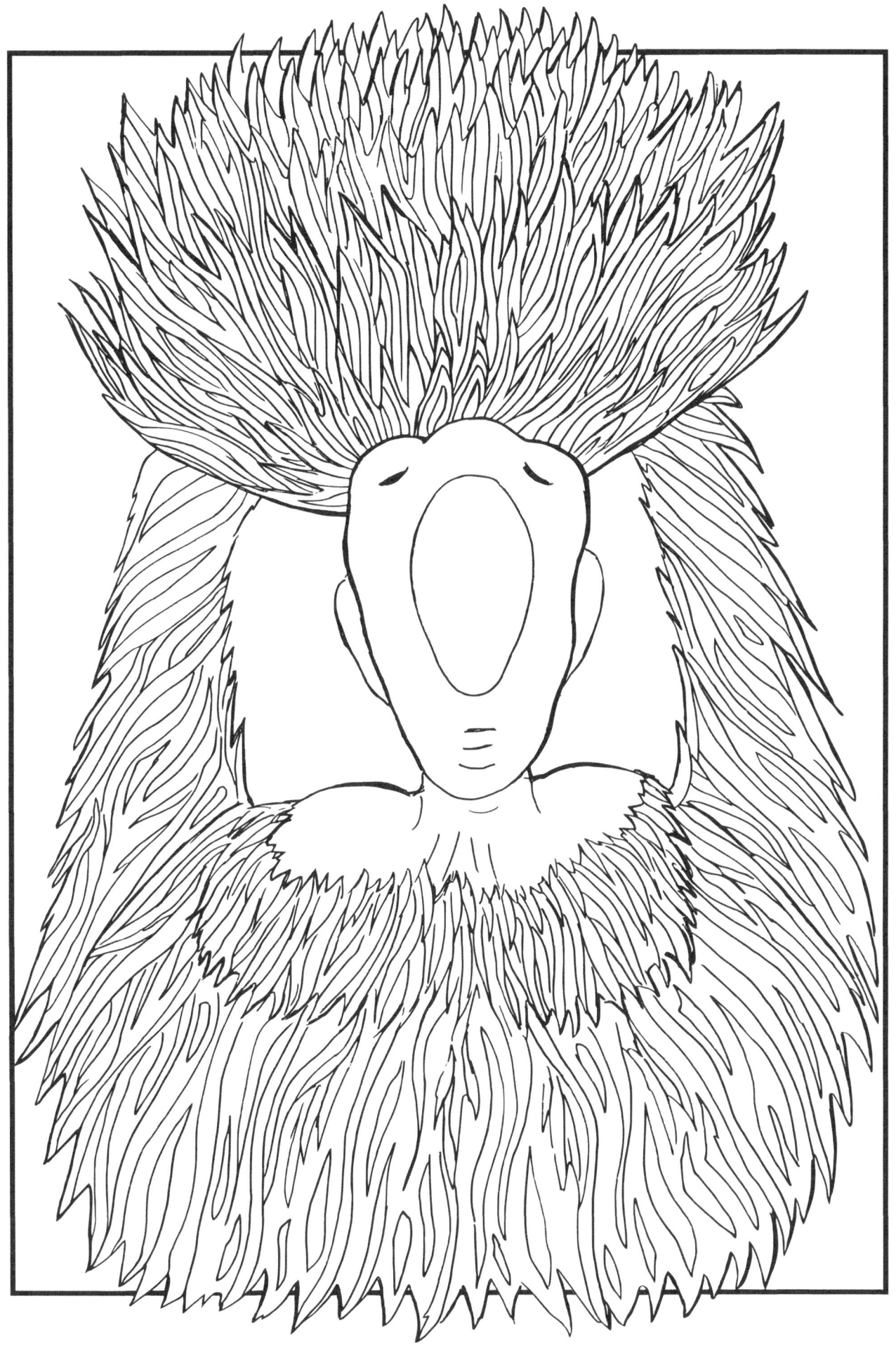

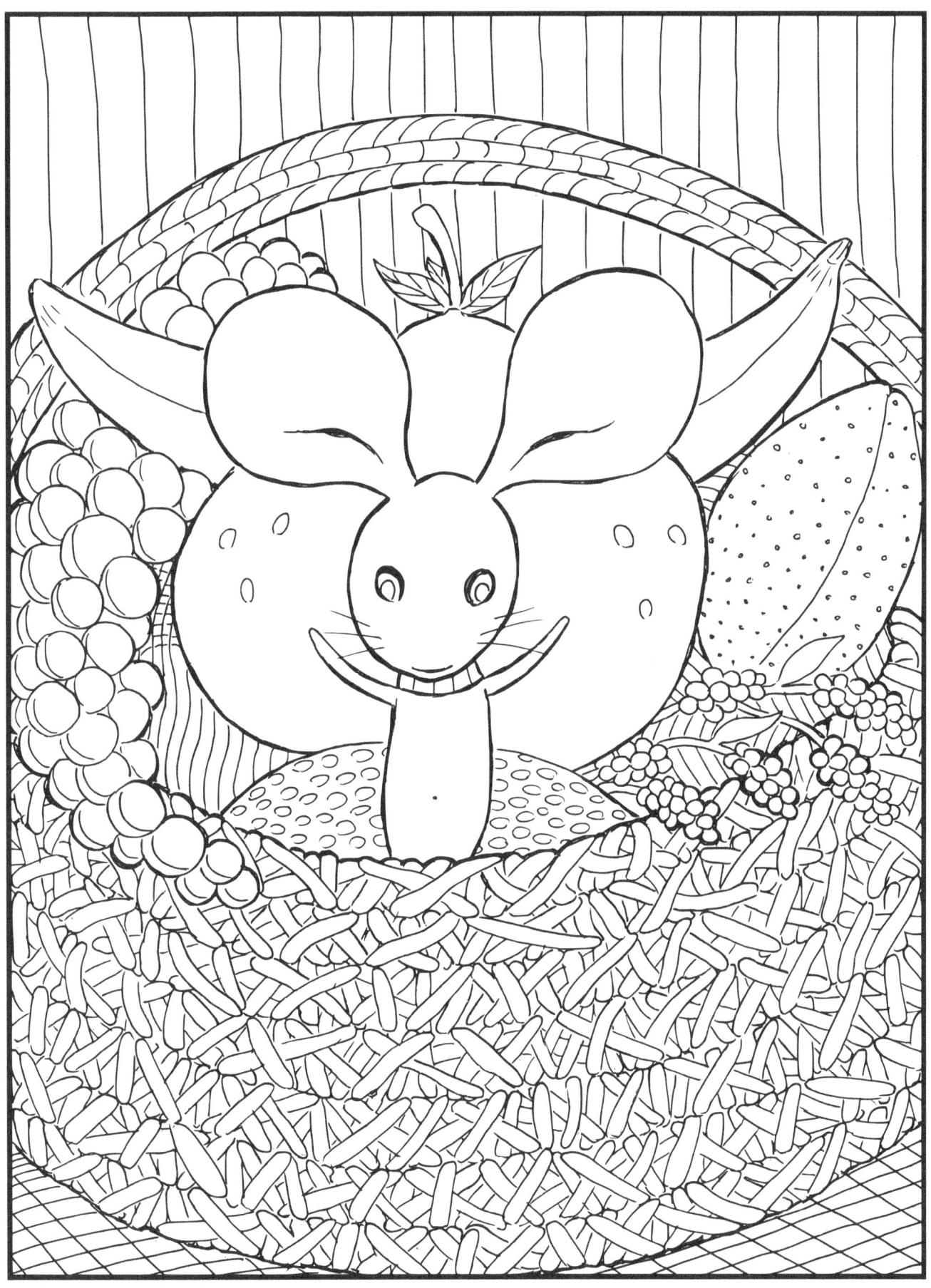

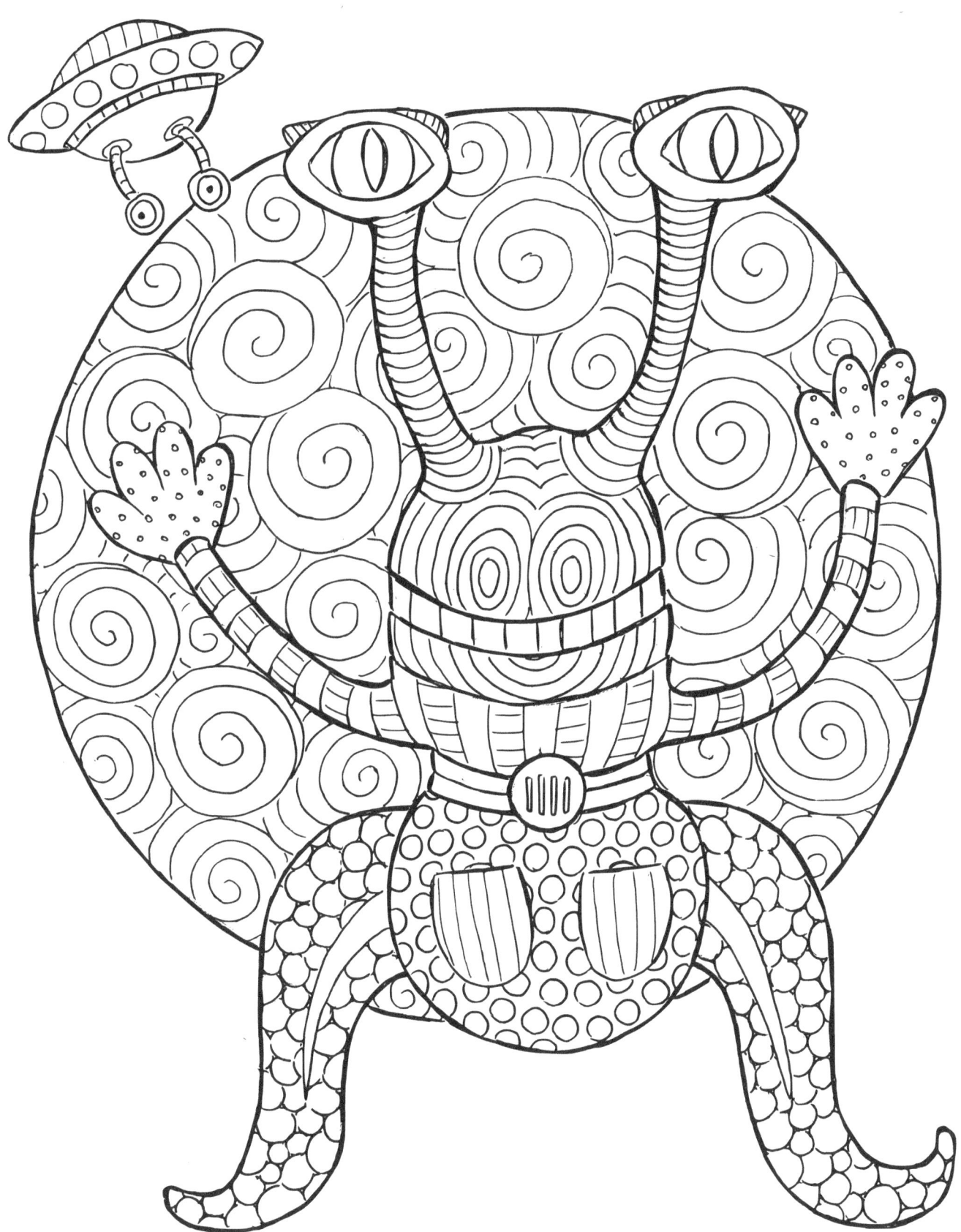

TEST AREA

Use this page to test out your colors and the way your media interacts with the paper.

For free coloring pages and artwork by me ('Trick) visit

www.TricksPlace.com

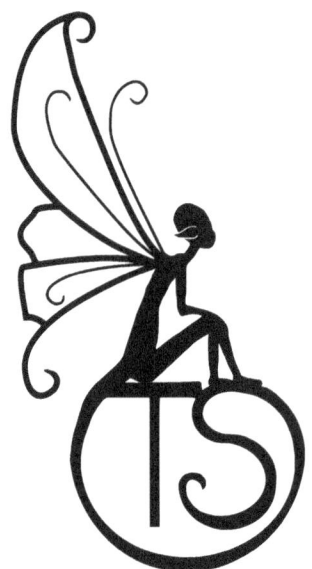

If you've enjoyed this coloring book please leave me a happy review on Amazon! Your help getting this book noticed will also allow me to create other unique coloring books.

And don't forget to connect with me at TricksPlace.com, follow me on facebook.com/tricksplace/ and also join the facebook group dedicated to sharing colored in pages from my books or website: facebook.com/groups/TricksPlaceColoring/

#tricksplace #multiviewcoloring